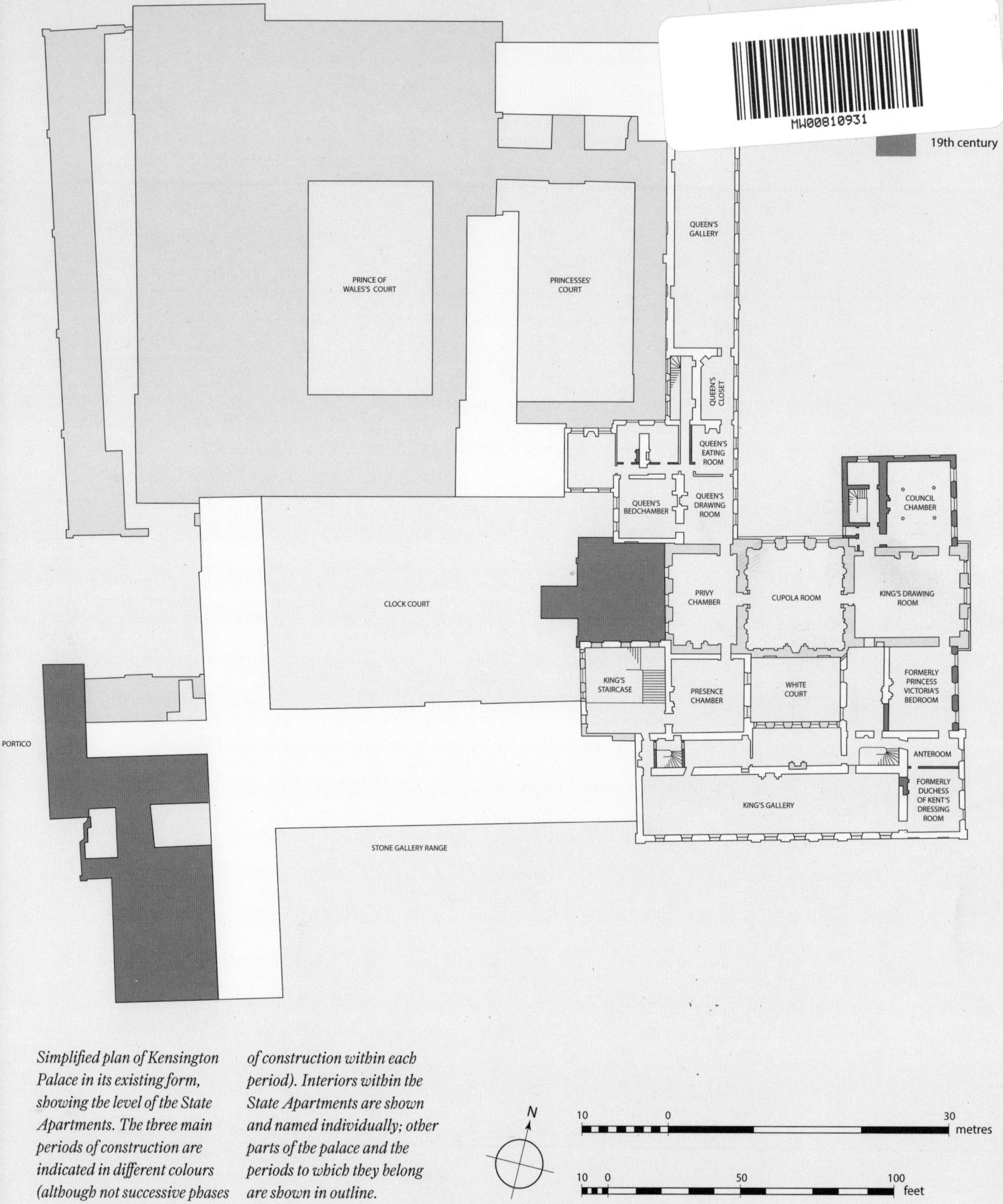

19th century
QUEEN'S GALLERY
PRINCE OF WALES'S COURT
PRINCESSES' COURT
QUEEN'S CLOSET
QUEEN'S EATING ROOM
QUEEN'S BEDCHAMBER
QUEEN'S DRAWING ROOM
COUNCIL CHAMBER
CLOCK COURT
PRIVY CHAMBER
CUPOLA ROOM
KING'S DRAWING ROOM
KING'S STAIRCASE
PRESENCE CHAMBER
WHITE COURT
FORMERLY PRINCESS VICTORIA'S BEDROOM
PORTICO
ANTEROOM
FORMERLY DUCHESS OF KENT'S DRESSING ROOM
KING'S GALLERY
STONE GALLERY RANGE
N
10 0 30 metres
10 0 50 100 feet

Simplified plan of Kensington Palace in its existing form, showing the level of the State Apartments. The three main periods of construction are indicated in different colours (although not successive phases of construction within each period). Interiors within the State Apartments are shown and named individually; other parts of the palace and the periods to which they belong are shown in outline.

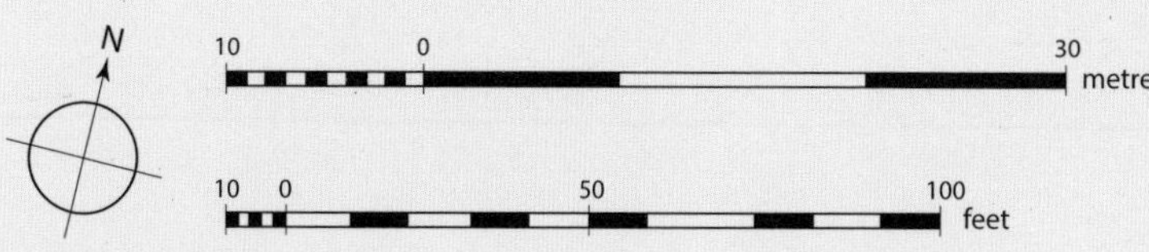

The Story of

Kensington Palace

The Story of Kensington Palace

Tracy Borman

MERRELL
LONDON • NEW YORK

In association with
Historic Royal Palaces

Contents

Introduction

Today Kensington Palace is synonymous with young royals, thanks to Princes William and Harry making it their home. It is also famous for being the residence of their mother, Diana, Princess of Wales, and visitors still flock to the palace in their hundreds of thousands to learn about her story. But Kensington's history stretches back much further than that. It boasts more than three centuries of continuous royal occupation, making it unique among the Historic Royal Palaces.

The first house to be built on the site in about 1616–18 was transformed into a royal palace by William and Mary towards the end of the seventeenth century. They were attracted by its location in what was then a small village to the west of London, with easy access to the capital but with much cleaner air. This remained its greatest advantage for the following two centuries, before it was overtaken by London's rapid expansion. Kensington Palace and its gardens are now surrounded by the bustling city, yet it still offers the same privacy and tranquillity that so appealed to its original royal owners.

Even after its conversion into a royal residence, the palace remained a rather unprepossessing building, fashioned out of reddish-grey brick and partially obscured by the trees and shrubberies that surround it. But this belied its architectural significance, for it was shaped and decorated by some of the country's leading architects, artists, craftsmen and designers, and is now a major national monument.

The palace's social and political significance is arguably even greater. Since 1689, by which time the original house had been sufficiently extended to accommodate William and Mary, the palace has played host to some of the most fascinating and important personalities and events in the long history of the royal family.

Kensington was the birthplace and childhood home of Queen Victoria, and it was here that she held her first council meeting as monarch. During the previous century, after the death of George II (the last reigning monarch to live there), Kensington had been divided up into apartments for the younger generation of the royal family, an arrangement that continues today. From the late nineteenth century onwards, it became a historic visitor attraction, a museum and home to the Royal Ceremonial Dress Collection. Today Kensington Palace is managed by Historic Royal Palaces and attracts more than 600,000 visitors a year, while continuing to be an important residence for members of the royal family.

1. The South Front of Kensington Palace, a favoured residence of five sovereigns and a royal home for more than three centuries.

This book tells the story of Kensington from private residence to modern-day royal palace. Its history is set against the backdrop of social and political events that shaped both Britain and its monarchy: from the Jacobite uprisings of the mid-eighteenth century to the rise of industrialization in the nineteenth, and the turbulence of world war in the twentieth.

Central to Kensington's significance is its modesty. In the domestic surrounds of the palace is revealed a more informal side to the royal family than is evident in the grander London residences. Here, the monarchy evolved and modernized in tandem with the times. The story of Kensington is, in short, the story of the modern monarchy.

Life at Court

The royal court was both the household of the reigning monarch and the centre of political life. It was also where fortunes – even lives – were won and lost. For centuries, it had been filled with ambitious men and women, all eager to make themselves pleasing to the king or queen so that they could share in the riches and power of their patronage.

Each palace was built around the monarch and designed to emphasize their magnificence. At the heart of every palace was a suite of rooms known as the Privy Chamber, or private apartments of the king or queen. Admittance to these was reserved for only those of the highest rank or favour. Beyond were the public rooms of court – the King's and Queen's Staircases, the Guard Chamber, the Presence or Audience Chamber, and the chapel – through which the monarch would regularly progress, besieged by place-seekers all the way (fig. 3).

The lives and routines of the monarchs who lived at Kensington were dictated by the same conventions as at the other royal residences. Most of these had been in place since the Middle Ages and were part of a bewildering array of elaborate ceremony, protocol and bureaucracy.

Responsibility for managing the monarch's servants, goods and houses across the country was assigned to three vast court departments, headed by the Lord Chamberlain, the Lord Steward and the Master of the Horse. Of these, the Lord Chamberlain's department was the most prestigious as it was responsible for the 'above stairs' staff. The Lord Steward managed the 'below stairs' department, including the kitchens and other service areas. The Master of the Horse, meanwhile, was in charge of the monarch's horses, transport and much recreational, ceremonial and military activity. Each of these positions still exists within the Royal Household today.

An additional department, the Bedchamber, came into existence from the early seventeenth century. Headed by the Groom of the Stool – the most prestigious courtier of all – this looked after the practical and ceremonial service of the monarch in both their 'public' bedchamber and the private rooms beyond (fig. 2). The title derived from the royal 'stool', or enclosed chamber pot, for which the groom was responsible.

The royal court was constantly on the move between the palaces in London and other parts of the kingdom – and, during the early Georgian period, Hanover, Germany. Early in its history as a royal residence, Kensington was established as a summer retreat, to which the king or queen would move after the end of each Parliament season.

2. *(above) Detail from the King's Staircase mural, showing Mehemet (in the blue cloak) and Mustapha (with the turban and white beard), George I's two Turkish Grooms of the Chamber. Their intimacy with the King aroused much envy at court.*

3. *(opposite)* The Great Staircase, Kensington Palace *by Richard Reeve after Charles Wild, from W.H. Pyne's* History of the Royal Residences, *1819. All the great and good of Georgian London would have climbed up these stairs to visit the King.*

At a convenient distance from the city, and – at least until well into the nineteenth century – a tranquil rural location, it was an ideal place for them to enjoy greater relaxation and privacy than at St James's Palace or Whitehall Palace, which were the focus of royal government (fig. 4).

When William and Mary stayed at Kensington for any period longer than two days, the senior officers and many other servants at court moved there with them. In 1699 the Lord Chamberlain laid down a set of rules stipulating that he himself, the Groom of the Stool, the Master of the Horse, the Keeper of the Privy Purse and the Gentleman and Groom of the Bedchamber should be in attendance on the King at all times. When the court was at St James's or Whitehall, many of these attendants could live in their own lodgings nearby, but this was not possible at Kensington, which in those days was situated beyond commuting distance from central London.

These servants were therefore assigned lodgings at the palace, and there was fierce competition to secure the most comfortable. Highly favoured courtiers such as Hans Willem Bentinck, 1st Earl of Portland and the great favourite of William III, enjoyed luxurious suites of rooms complete with their own servants, while others had to put up with cramped and uncomfortable apartments (fig. 5). George II's long-suffering mistress Henrietta Howard complained that her room at Kensington was so damp that 'the floor produced a constant crop of mushrooms'.

4. View of the East or Park Front of Kensington Palace from beyond the Great Basin, after John Rocque, 1736, showing groups of courtiers enjoying the palace gardens.

5. Hans Willem Bentinck, 1st Earl of Portland, from the studio of Hyacinthe Rigaud, 1698–99. The Earl of Portland was William III's chief favourite, and held the important office of Groom of the Stool.

The monarch lived according to an ordered, often monotonous daily routine. This began with the long-established dressing ritual in the Little Bedchamber, where the designated staff handed the king or queen a succession of garments in strictly regulated order. They might then have received high-ranking visitors in the Great Bedchamber; this ceremony was called the *levée* (literally, 'getting up') after that of the French court, and had been established in England under Charles II. If they were attending to state and political business, the monarch might then have conducted meetings with their ministers in an adjoining closet or 'cabinet' (from which the modern political body takes its name). On less frequent occasions, they attended meetings of the Privy Council, a group of high-ranking advisers established by Henry VIII. At Kensington, this met in a dedicated Council Chamber in the north-eastern pavilion.

When the king or queen received foreign dignitaries and ambassadors, they would do so in the State Apartments. Such occasions would be laden with elaborate ceremony, all designed to project their majesty and magnificence so that they would be reported back to their

6. Engraving after Thomas Rowlandson and Augustus Charles Pugin depicting a 'Drawing Room' at St James's Palace, 1809.

rival monarchs. Dinners would often be staged in honour of foreign guests. These meals usually began in the middle of the afternoon and could last for several hours. They tended to be held in the private apartments, with any necessary furniture being brought in for the occasion. Thanks to detailed records kept by the Lord Steward's department, we know that a vast range and quantity of food and drink were brought to Kensington on a regular basis. This was consumed by the monarch and their household, either at formal dinners or at more intimate gatherings.

Once or twice a week, the sovereign would hold an audience, usually in the Presence Chamber, so that their subjects could see and perhaps talk to them. During William and Mary's reign, courtiers and high-ranking members of society could meet their King or Queen at the regular gatherings held in the Queen's Drawing Room. The relative informality of the Queen's Apartments made these particularly enjoyable occasions. In later reigns, the 'Drawing Room' was to become the main public event of court life (figs. 6 and 7).

There were also plenty of events for entertainment, usually to mark an occasion such as the King's birthday or the arrival of an important guest. The most spectacular of these were balls, and a description of one in January 1694 gives a flavour of what they were like: 'Saturday night last was a great entertainment made for the Prince of Baden at Kensington, where was dancing and gaming, and a great supper; and banquets of sweetmeats all common to such as were admitted to be spectators. And I was informed by one that was present, that he supposed there could not be less than 1000 persons, but it was 5 of the clock in the morning before some of them could get home.'

The death of Queen Mary at the end of that year sparked a decline in social activity at Kensington, but from the late 1690s musical and theatrical entertainments became popular there. In 1698 a stage was fitted up for 'a performance of music before his Majesty at Kensington', and furniture was ordered for 'the new theatre at Kensington'.

But court life at Kensington lost much of its sparkle in the following century. In his 'Epistle to a Lady' (1714), the poet and dramatist John Gay scorned the monotony of life at the Georgian court:

> Pensive each night, from room to room I walk'd,
> To one I bow'd, and with another talk'd;
> Enquir'd what news, or such a Lady's name,
> And did the next day, and the next, the same.

When Henrietta Howard finally escaped court in 1734 and moved to her Thames-side villa in Twickenham, another of her literary friends, Alexander Pope, observed, 'There is a greater court now at Marble Hill than at Kensington, and God knows when it will end.'

7. Gentleman's court suit, c. 1760–80. Attendance at court was not by invitation but was open to anyone sufficiently well dressed to be admitted by the footmen.

Kensington before the Palace

Today Kensington is a thriving and densely populated suburb of west London, and one of the capital's most prestigious addresses. But when the first house was built on the site of the modern-day palace, the area was a tranquil backwater, favoured for the cleaner air that its residents could enjoy, compared to the stench of central London.

Evidence of early human settlement in Kensington is sparse, but a number of archaeological finds suggest that the area may have been a permanent settlement from the Bronze Age, some 2800 years ago. Iron Age occupation has also been identified, with the discovery of a coin hoard at the north-western corner of Kensington Gardens and some small pieces of pottery close to the modern-day Orangery. The Roman conquest of Britain in the first century AD and the establishment of Londinium as an important and populous city prompted the building of two roads leading west out of the city. These provided a key means of communication and supply between London and the Kensington area.

It was not until Anglo-Saxon times, from the fifth to the eleventh century, that the name Kensington was established. The settlement is recorded as 'Chenesiton' in Domesday Book (fig. 8). The name possibly derives from its links to nearby Chelsea or 'Chelchehithe', meaning 'chalk and landing place'. By 1086 the estate was in the hands of Aubrey de Vere, chamberlain to William the Conqueror's wife, Matilda. It

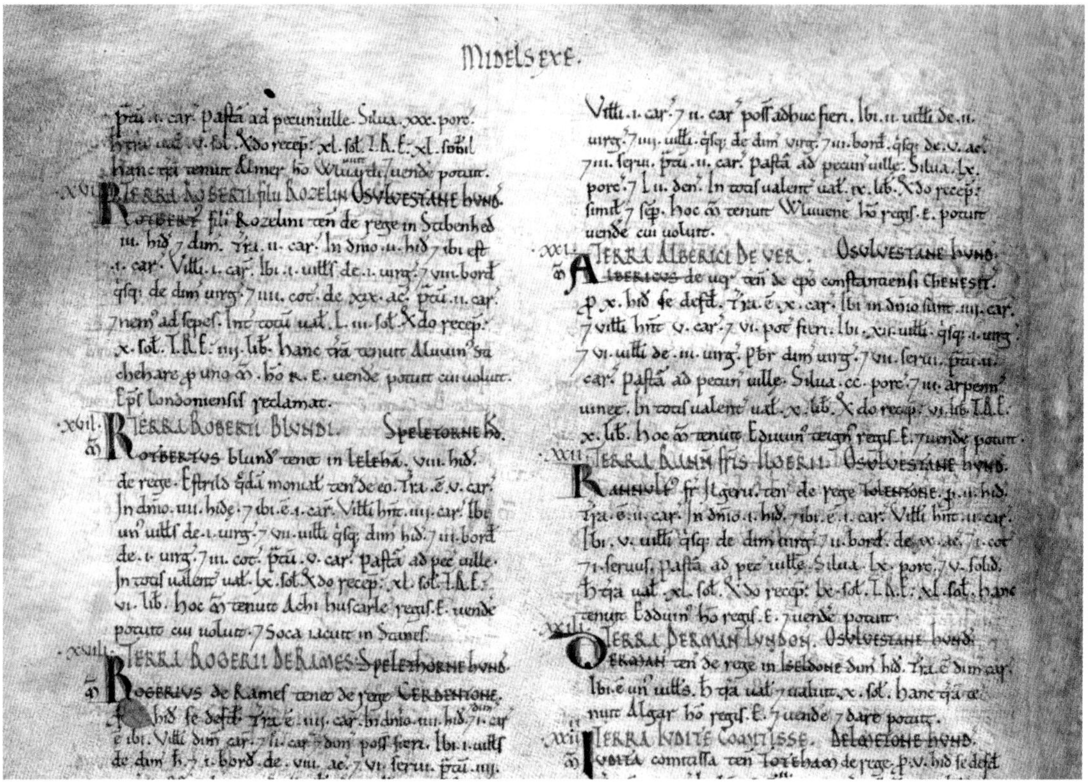

8. The entry in Domesday Book showing the manor of Kensington ('Chenesiton'). The property is identified in red capitals towards the top of the second column as the Terra Alberici De Ver *('Land of Aubrey de Vere'). De Vere's descendants retained links with Kensington until the 1520s.*

9. View of the south front of Holland House by the architect and antiquarian John Buckler, 1812. Built in about 1606–14 by Sir Walter Cope, the exterior of the house remained largely unaltered until its partial destruction by incendiary bombs in 1940.

was from de Vere that the later Earls of Oxford were descended, and Kensington remained in their ownership for more than four centuries, during which time it became a wealthy manor with extensive lands.

The Dissolution of the Monasteries by Henry VIII (1509–47) had a profound impact on Kensington and its surroundings, devaluing the land so that it was affordable for the new aspirational courtiers who emerged during the Tudor period. The manor transferred from the de Vere family to a succession of different owners during the sixteenth century. Meanwhile, Henry VIII decided to indulge his passion for hunting by creating a new hunting park that consumed much of the land nearby. Hyde Park, as it was later known, is the largest of the four Royal Parks that form a chain from the entrance of Kensington Palace to Buckingham Palace.

The creation of Hyde Park enhanced Kensington's appeal to wealthy courtiers looking for a home with clean air and water, and spacious grounds where they could take their leisure and entertain. The village was also ideally located on the road that led directly to the palace of Whitehall, where the royal court was often in residence. In the late sixteenth century, when Henry VIII's daughter Elizabeth I (1558–1603)

10. Reconstructed view of Sir George Coppin's house at Kensington, built c. *1616–18.*

was on the throne, Kensington became established as one of the most desirable of all the new London suburbs that were beginning to emerge.

Between 1605 and 1618, three grand houses were built in the area: Cope Castle (later named Holland House), Campden House and what came to be known as Nottingham House (fig. 9). The latter was built by Sir George Coppin, a self-made and ambitious social climber who served the powerful Cecil family at court. His new Kensington home took just two years to build and was completed in 1618. Coppin moved in straight away, but did not enjoy his new home for long because he died two years later. His architectural legacy was much more enduring, however. Nottingham House became the nucleus of the royal palace that stands on the site today.

Coppin's new house was built in the latest style favoured by the early Stuart elite. These suburban houses – or villas, as they became known – were intended for retreat, recreation and family life. As such, they were relatively small and compact in comparison to the grander country estates that were scattered across the kingdom. Nottingham House adhered to the new 'H-plan' design, rather than the medieval arrangement of rooms around courtyards. Built principally in brick, it boasted large bay windows at the centre of all four façades (fig. 10).

In 1624 Nottingham House was purchased by Sir Heneage Finch, a successful lawyer who held a string of prestigious posts, including Serjeant-at-Law and later Speaker of Parliament. On his death in 1631, he bequeathed the house to his second wife, Elizabeth, who lived there with their two daughters for the next thirty years. Although this would prove to be one of the most turbulent periods in British history, during which the country was torn apart by civil war, Elizabeth Finch and her children continued to live quietly at their house.

The population of Kensington village had continued to rise during the first half of the seventeenth century. The famous diarist Samuel Pepys was a regular visitor to the village during the 1660s, and was a great admirer of the Finches' garden (fig. 11). On one occasion in 1664, he remarked upon what 'a mighty fine cool place it is, with a great laver of water in the middle, and the bravest place for music I ever heard'.

11. Samuel Pepys, whose diaries provide such vivid anecdotes about London life during the reign of Charles II. Pepys visited Kensington village on many occasions during the 1660s, and his descriptions of the gardens are particularly useful. Portrait by John Hayls, 1666.

By this time, Nottingham House was under the ownership of Sir Heneage's eldest son and namesake, later 1st Earl of Nottingham. When the Great Fire swept across London in 1666, Sir Heneage climbed to the roof of his house, which offered an excellent vantage point over the city. He described the scene of devastation in a letter to his brother-in-law, Viscount Conway: 'Had your Lordship been at Kensington, you would have thought for five days together, for so long the Fire lasted, it had been Doomesday and that the heavens themselves had been on fire, and the fearfull cryes and howlings of undone people did much encrease the resemblance. My walkes and Gardens were almost covered with the ashes of papers, linens, etc. and pieces of ceeling and plaster work blown hither by the Tempest.'

12. (top, left) Lady Essex Finch by Peter Lely, c. 1675. Lady Essex was the first wife of Daniel Finch and died in childbirth in 1684. Her husband subsequently married Anne Hatton, by whom he had twenty-two children; at least thirteen survived to adulthood.

13. (top, right) This beautiful bed was made in about 1685, almost certainly for Daniel Finch at Nottingham House. Fittingly, in 1974 it was bought by the Dutch palace of Het Loo – one of William and Mary's former residences – and is shown here displayed in the bedchamber that Mary used as Princess of Orange.

14. (above) Daniel Finch, 2nd Earl of Nottingham, by Sir Godfrey Kneller, c. 1720. A Privy Counsellor to Charles II, Finch lived at Nottingham House with his second wife and their large family. He helped to pave the way for William and Mary to take the throne, and sold Nottingham House to them in 1689.

After Lord Nottingham's death in 1682, Nottingham House passed to his eldest son, Daniel, 2nd Earl of Nottingham, who like his father had a successful career in law, administration and politics, and was a Privy Counsellor to Charles II (figs. 12, 13 and 14). He and his second wife, Anne Hatton, had twenty-two children, at least thirteen of whom survived to adulthood; Nottingham House must have become increasingly cramped as their family grew. The political situation also made Lord Nottingham inclined to sell his Kensington home. The accession of the staunchly Catholic James II in 1685 troubled him greatly, as it did large swathes of the new King's subjects. Along with many other Anglican loyalists, Lord Nottingham had begun to look to James's eldest daughter, Mary, and her husband, Prince William of Orange, to replace the King. However, when William was 'invited' to invade England in 1688, Lord Nottingham held back, feeling unable to participate in violence against his anointed sovereign (fig. 15).

The so-called 'Glorious Revolution' proved peaceful, but Lord Nottingham was marked as a sympathizer of James and did not thrive in the new political climate. When William and Mary visited Nottingham House in May 1689 and the King took a liking to it, Lord Nottingham was all too pleased to sell. This marked the beginning of Kensington's long history as a royal palace.

15. The Landing of William Prince of Orange, in Torbay, on November the 5th 1688, *after James Northcote, 1801. William arrived with 14,000 troops, but the 'Glorious Revolution' that brought him and his wife, Mary, to the throne was a peaceful one.*

Kensington under William and Mary, 1689–1702

On being offered the Crown in February 1689, William and Mary soon realized that they were in urgent need of suitable accommodation (figs. 17 and 18). The abolition of the monarchy in 1649 had resulted in the sale and destruction of many of the ancient royal palaces. Most were beyond salvage by the time of the Restoration in 1660. The once lavish royal apartments at the Tower of London had fallen into a dire state of repair, as had Greenwich Palace, which Charles II (1660–85) tried and failed to restore to its former splendour. Only the vast, sprawling palace of Whitehall – largely the creation of Henry VIII – remained habitable. Charles therefore re-established this as the principal royal residence in London, and established his brother (and successor) James at nearby St James's Palace.

But neither palace was considered suitable by William and Mary. St James's was too closely associated with the king they had ousted, and Whitehall was in the midst of smoke-filled London. It was also prone to flooding and damp, which presented a real problem for the new King, who suffered from chronic asthma and had already admitted that his condition was 'getting worse in this climate'. Besides, Whitehall was too formal for William and Mary's tastes: what they needed was to establish their reign in altogether more comfortable surroundings.

Just nine days into their reign, the couple visited Hampton Court, Henry VIII's magnificent Thames-side palace close to Kingston. They

16. Bird's-eye view of Hampton Court Palace from the east, painted by Leonard Knyff in the early years of Queen Anne's reign. The lavish new apartments built for William and Mary can be seen in the foreground.

17. (above, left) William III by Sir Godfrey Kneller. This was one of a pair of portraits of William and his wife, Mary, that were painted in 1690. It was hung in the Council Chamber at Kensington Palace.

18. (above) Mary II by Sir Godfrey Kneller, 1690. Like her husband, William, the new Queen is shown in her coronation robes. Both paintings became the official portraits of the dual monarchs and were much copied for British embassies abroad.

fell in love with it immediately, and, according to a contemporary commentator, William 'found the air of Hampton Court agreed so well with him that he resolved to live the greatest part of the year there'. Much as they liked the Tudor palace, it was hopelessly outdated, so they set about an ambitious programme of remodelling. By 1698 Hampton Court had been transformed into a baroque masterpiece that proclaimed the stately face of the new parliamentary monarchy (fig. 16).

Nonetheless, for all its splendour and modern comforts, the palace lay several hours' distance from the heart of government, which made it impractical as a year-round residence for the King and Queen. One of the most influential ministers, the Marquess of Halifax, complained that 'the King's inaccessibleness and living so at Hampton Court altogether, and at as so active a time ruined all business'.

19. Sir Christopher Wren, with his most celebrated work, St Paul's Cathedral, in the background. Wren was commissioned by William and Mary in 1689 to transform Nottingham House into a royal residence. He retained the original house and added a 'pavilion' at each corner. His design influenced the architectural development of the palace for many years to come. Portrait by John Closterman, c. *1690.*

20. Bridget Holmes, Necessary Woman to James II and William III, by John Riley, 1686. She is shown brandishing a broom and playing a game with a Page of the Backstairs.

It was while he was riding to Hampton Court from the city that King William discovered the perfect solution. Nottingham House may have been small compared to other potential royal residences, but the fact that it stood on a relatively flat site made it ripe for extension. Its situation on the edge of Hyde Park further enhanced its appeal because, as royal property, this offered the King and Queen control over the views to the east, as well as the potential to extend the grounds. By mid-June 1689, the deal had been struck with Lord Nottingham, but it was not until the following March that he received 'payment in full of £20,000 for the purchase of his Lordship's House, gardens and lands lying and being within the walls of Kensington in Middlesex'.

In her memoirs, Queen Mary reflected, 'The misfortune of the King's health which hindered him living at Whitehall, put people out of humour, being here naturally lazy. The King had bought Lord Nottingham's house to please them.' But she and William were determined to make a virtue out of necessity, and soon set about transforming their new home into a palace – albeit a modest one. They took up residence at nearby Holland House while the works were under way so that they could keep a close eye on progress.

William and Mary enlisted the services of the most celebrated architect of the day. Sir Christopher Wren had been appointed by Charles II to advise on the rebuilding of London after the Great Fire of 1666 (fig. 19). Much of the modern cityscape was created by Wren, including his crowning glory, St Paul's Cathedral. Nevertheless, his appointment by the new sovereigns was by no means a foregone conclusion. He was very much associated with the old regime, and William might well have awarded the commission to a Dutchman, as he did the Superintendency of the Royal Gardens. But Wren succeeded in ingratiating himself with the royal couple, and they soon set him to work at Kensington.

Wren's challenge was to create a new royal home that, though modest, would still be able to house the functions of the court and political gatherings. As well as the King and Queen, it would need to accommodate a large household of officials and servants (fig. 20). Above all, it had to be executed quickly and economically (fig. 21). Wren's response was typically pragmatic. Rather than demolishing the existing house, he used it as the centrepiece of the new palace, adding a rectangular block or 'pavilion' at each corner (figs. 22 and 25). This decision would affect the subsequent history and configuration of the palace to the present day.

In order to adhere to the requirement of economy, the palace was mainly built from brick, which was far cheaper than stone. Fashionable sash windows were used only at first-floor level, as these were expensive. The work was paid for out of the annual income of £600,000 that Parliament granted to the new sovereigns in 1689.

Queen Mary took a keen interest in the progress of her new palace and regularly visited the site. Thanks in no small part to her constant chivvying, progress was rapid. But it came at a terrible cost. In November 1689, part of the new building work collapsed, killing one of the workmen and injuring several more. This was soon exaggerated by the press, which reported, 'The new apartment ... all of a sudden without any warning given fell flat to the

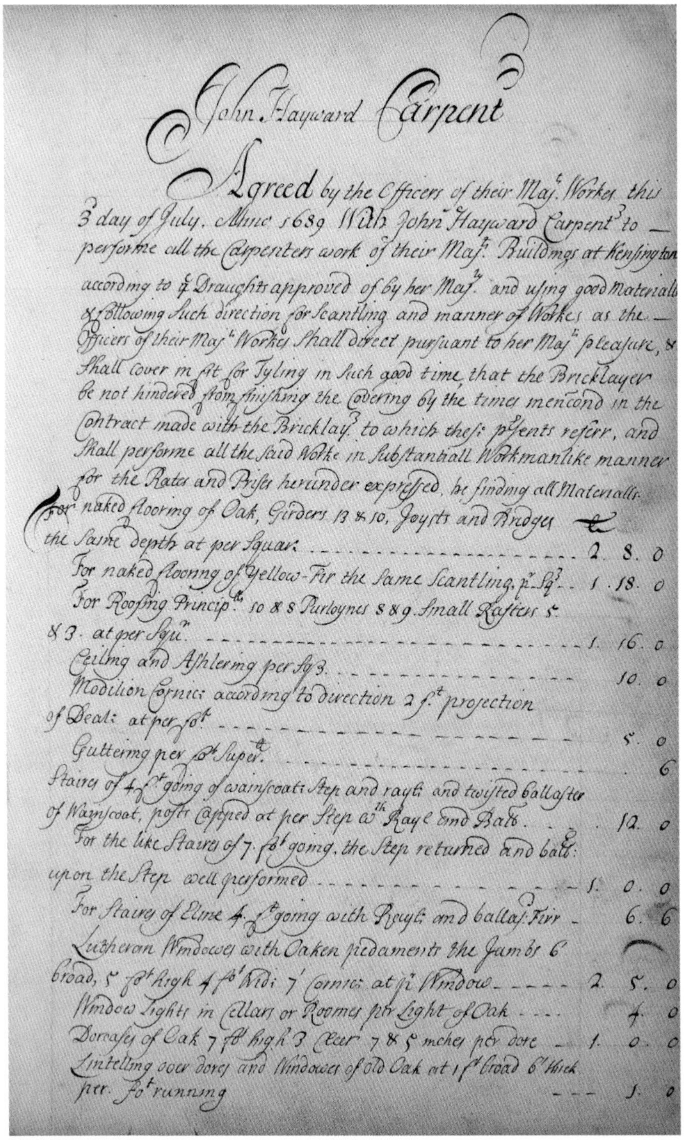
John Hayward Carpent

Agreed by the Officers of their Maj.ts Workes this 3d day of July. Anno 1689 With John Hayward Carpent.r to performe all the Carpenters work of their Maj.ts Buildings at Kensington according to ye Draughts approved of by her Maj.ty and using good Materialls & following such direction for Scantling and manner of Workes as the Officers of their Maj.ts Workes shall direct pursuant to her Maj.ts pleasure, & shall cover in fit for Tyling in such good time, that the Bricklayer be not hindered from finishing the Covering by the times mencond in the Contract made with the Bricklay.r to which these p.sents referr, and shall performe all the said Worke in substantiall Workmanlike manner for the Rates and Prises hereunder expressed, he finding all Materialls.

	£	s	d
For naked flooring of Oak, Girders 13 & 10, Joysts and Bridges the same depth at per Squar:	2	8	0
For naked flooring of Yellow-Firr the same Scantling, p.r Sq.r	1	18	0
For Roofing Princip.lls 10 & 8 Purloynes 8 & 9. Small Rafters 5 & 3. at per Squ.r	1	16	0
Ceiling and Ashlering per Sq.r		10	0
Modilion Cornice according to direction 2 f.t projection of Deal: at per fo.t		5	0
Guttering per fo.t Super.			6
Staires of 4 f.t going of wainscoat: Step and rayl: and twisted ballaster of Wainscoat, posts Capped at per Step w.th Rayl and Bals.		12	0
For the like Staires of 7. fo.t going. the Step returned and bals: upon the Step well performed	1	0	0
For Staires of Elme 4. f.t going with Rayl: and ballas: Firr		6	6
Lutheran Windowes with Oaken pedaments the Jambs 6 broad, 5 fo.t high 4 fo.t wide 7' Cornice: at p.r Window	2	5	0
Window Lights in Cellars or Roomes per Light of Oak		4	0
Dorcases of Oak 7 fo.t high 3 Cleer 7 & 5 inches per dore	1	0	0
Lintelling over dores and Windowes of old Oak at 1 f.t broad 6" thick per. fo.t running		1	0

21. The contract between John Hayward and the Office of Works, signed in July 1689, for all the carpentry required to transform Nottingham House for William and Mary. It also testifies to the speed at which Hayward and his fellow craftsmen were obliged to work.

22. *(right)* The North side of The Kings House at Kinsington, *as depicted by the draughtsman and engraver Sutton Nicholls between 1689 and 1694. The early seventeenth-century house can be seen in the centre, with the new 'pavilions' added for William and Mary to either side.*

ground and was killed as I am told 7 or 8 workmen and labourers'; the writer added that 'the Queen had been in the apartment but a very little before, but is mighty troubled at the misfortune'. The latter part of the report was true, at least. Mary was still guilt-ridden when she wrote her memoirs, recalling that she would 'go often to Kensington to hasten the workmen and I was too impatient to be at that place, imagining to find more ease there. This I often reproved myself for and at last it pleased God to show me the uncertainty of all things below: for part of the house which was new built fell down.'

Work soon resumed, and by the end of November detailed plans were being made for the palace's furnishing. This process was managed by the Great Wardrobe, a vast government department that had been responsible since the Middle Ages for storing and managing the royal clothes, furnishings and other goods. New items were ordered from the

23. *(left) Commissioned by William III for Kensington Palace in 1698, this table by Andrew Moore is one of the most magnificent surviving examples of the fashion for silver furniture, which spread to England from the court of Louis XIV at Versailles.*

24. *(below) Bust of a man by John Nost the Elder,* c. 1700. *This luxurious sculpture was displayed in the King's Gallery. The figure has traditionally been identified as a favourite personal servant of William III.*

leading furniture makers of the day, but, still with an eye to economy, the couple also made use of existing pieces from Holland House and other royal residences (fig. 23).

On Christmas Eve 1689, some six months after the works began, William and Mary moved into their new home. This marked the beginning of more than three centuries of continuous royal occupation at Kensington – something that few other palaces can boast. Although works continued for several more months, the new palace was habitable enough for the King and Queen to live in relative comfort (if not quite peace) with their household.

Thanks to Wren's decision to retain the original house, Kensington had little of the symmetry that would have been expected of a newly built palace. The main entrance, which lay on the west side of the complex, was marked only by a modest timber porte cochère (coach

25. *(left) Kensington Palace from the south by Noel Gasselin, 1693. This early view shows the gables and central turret of Sir George Coppin's house in the centre of Wren's pavilions.*

26. View of the Great Court (or Clock Court), looking west. Designed by Wren, it was completed by April 1690.

gate) of Tuscan columns. This opened into the Stone Gallery, a 55-metre-long (180 ft) enclosed corridor within a narrow block that ran eastwards to the south-western pavilion, with lodgings for important courtiers above and behind it. Facing this to the north was the Great Court (now known as Clock Court), which was entered through an archway with a clock tower above and enclosed to the north by a range of service buildings, including new kitchens (fig. 26).

The far end of the Stone Gallery opened at the foot of the Great (or King's) Stair, which led to the grandest rooms in the building: the State Apartments. Situated in the south-western pavilion, these are where the formal routines of court life and royal business were conducted. The layout of the rooms was dictated by the need to control access to the sovereign, while providing areas for meetings with ministers and other officials, as well as a degree of personal privacy. The same linear formation that had been used in royal palaces since Tudor times was adopted at Kensington, with a sequence of spaces through which a visitor progressed. The further they were allowed to advance towards the room that the King occupied, the higher ranking or more favoured they were.

The first room in the sequence tended to be the Guard Chamber, staffed by the Yeomen of the Guard, a military unit established by Henry VII (1485–1509) to safeguard his person. Beyond that lay the Presence Chamber, at the far end of which the sovereign sat enthroned to receive important guests. Those who were more highly favoured still would be admitted to the Privy Chamber, which – as the name suggests – was a suite of more private rooms. These, too, were laid out in sequence, with a Great Bedchamber followed by a Little Bedchamber, adjoining which was one or more 'closets': small rooms for study, business or recreation. The King's Privy Lodgings lay beyond and below the Privy Chamber, and were reached by the 'Privy Stair'.

The Queen's Apartments lay in the north-western pavilion and included a drawing room, dressing room, closets, bedchamber and eating room, with a separate back staircase (fig. 27). The apartments extended into the old Nottingham House, which contained the Presence Chamber that Mary shared with her husband. However, in the summer of 1690, with her apartments barely complete, the Queen set about

27. (above) The Queen's Eating Room, used by William and Mary for informal dining. In Mary's time it was furnished with walnut chairs and stools, crimson damask curtains, and screens to keep out draughts.

28. (left) The wing commissioned by Mary II to enlarge the Queen's Apartments at Kensington in 1690. The doorway opens at the foot of the Queen's Staircase, providing access between the apartments and the gardens.

29. The Queen's Staircase, little changed since its construction in 1690–91.

extending them. A further ten bays were added to her pavilion to create a new gallery, grand staircase and lodgings for her maids of honour (fig. 28). This new building project may have been driven less by a genuine need for additional space than by Mary's more pressing need for diversion at a time of political and military insecurity. In March the ousted King James II (1685–88) had made a bid to regain his throne, and had landed in Ireland with the support of French troops. The Anglo-Dutch Wars were also still raging, and in June, King William had embarked on a campaign that culminated in a victory on the River Boyne.

Mary again proved impatient while the works were under way. As the sole Head of State in the King's absence, she was obliged to live mostly at Whitehall, but visited Kensington regularly. She kept her husband informed of progress, and on one occasion wrote with some frustration that 'the outside of the house is the fiddling work, which takes up more time that one can imagine, [and] while the scaffolds are up the windows must be boarded up'. The new, extended Queen's Apartments were finished in March 1691 at a cost of more than £60,000 – three times the purchase price of Nottingham House.

The extension comprised a long, narrow range of two floors over a basement. As usual, the most important rooms were upstairs and were accessible from the existing house, as well as via an external doorway and staircase (fig. 29). The largest room was the gallery, an impressive 26.4-metre-long (86½ ft) space that was inspired by the long galleries found in Tudor and Stuart mansions.

Mary's decorative and furnishing scheme for her new apartments was perhaps the most remarkable ever achieved at Kensington. Grinling Gibbons adorned the gallery with two carved and gilded

30. One of the two fireplaces and overmantels in the Queen's Gallery. The overmantel was made by the celebrated Dutch sculptor and carver Grinling Gibbons, and is a rare survival of the giltwood furniture used by Mary II to display porcelain.

overmantel mirror surrounds (fig. 30), and supplied two carved chimney pieces for the Queen's dressing room and closet. The highlight, though, was the Queen's extraordinary porcelain collection. Her knowledge of and love for porcelain and Oriental applied art had been inspired by her years in Holland, which then dominated control of Far Eastern trade. Some of the pieces she displayed at Kensington were brought over from the Dutch palaces; others were purchased new or inherited. They occupied five of Mary's new rooms, including the gallery, which housed no fewer than 154 pieces.

The Queen was not alone in her passion for porcelain. The author Daniel Defoe described 'the Custom or Humour, as I may call it, of furnishing houses with China-Ware, which increased to a strange degree afterwards, piling their China on the Tops of Cabinets, Scrutores [writing desks], and every Chimney-Piece, to the tops of the Ceilings, and even setting up shelves for their China-Ware'. Much of the remaining furnishings in Mary's apartments were also in an Oriental style, such as the Japanese lacquered furniture and the printed cottons from India. The crimson velvet hangings on the walls of the gallery must have created an effect that was extraordinarily rich and exotic, especially by candlelight.

Mary took up residence in her new apartments on 8 September 1691 and was joined two days later by William, newly returned from his military triumph. But they had barely had time to enjoy their refurbished home when disaster struck. On the night of 10 November 1691, the royal couple were woken by a noise that sounded like the firing of muskets. Fearing a plot, they were soon informed that a fire had broken out in the Stone Gallery, probably started by 'the carelessness

31. Engraving of 1678 showing a pump or 'engine', probably similar to those brought over from Whitehall to fight the fire at Kensington in 1691.

of a candle'. The palace was equipped only with 'a small engine to quench fire', and this soon proved inadequate. Soldiers from the nearby barracks did their best to douse the flames with water carried in broken-open bottles from the beer cellar, but the blaze rapidly took hold. During the two hours that it took for more sophisticated fire-fighting equipment to arrive from Whitehall, the King ordered the removal of furniture and other items from the royal apartments into the gardens, including the Queen's porcelain and even some Dutch cheeses (fig. 31).

Mary still feared 'some treason', but her husband 'smiled at the suggestion [and] cheered her Majesty up'. They stood together in the gardens for several hours until 'they perceived the Fire by the help that came in ... was gotten under Foot'. The Queen, who was greatly chastened by the experience, reflected, 'This had truly, I hoped, weaned me from the vanities I was most fond of, that is ease and good lodgings.'

By the following morning, the fire had been extinguished. Although the main house had been saved, the entire Stone Gallery range, including some important courtiers' apartments, had been gutted. The scale of the damage is revealed by the estimates that were drawn up for its repair, which included 59 chimney pieces, 156 windows and 372 sq. metres (4000 sq. ft) of glass. As well as making good the damage, the opportunity was taken to create a more imposing entrance to the royal apartments from the Great Court, and to improve and relocate the Guard Chamber.

32. Henry Wise by Sir Godfrey Kneller, c. 1715. Wise and George London were responsible for designing, creating and maintaining the gardens at Kensington during the reigns of William and Mary and Queen Anne.

At the same time, work was under way in the gardens. Both William and Mary had taken a keen interest in gardens during their years in Holland, and boasted considerable expertise in planting. They had improved the gardens at their residence of Honselaarsdijk and had created entirely new ones at the palace of Het Loo. Now that their new palace was complete, they were eager to see the gardens laid out according to the latest fashions.

Before work could begin, the King and Queen were obliged to purchase some additional land adjoining their estate to the south-west. This was so that a driveway could be built that led from the new front entrance of the house to the Hammersmith Road, without encroaching on the lawns to the south of the house, for which the couple had ambitious planting plans.

The bulk of the work seems to have taken place between 1690 and 1696. Again, it was Mary who was the driving force behind it. Daniel Defoe later claimed that, at Kensington, 'The first laying out of these

gardens was the design of the late Queen Mary, who finding the air agreed with, and was necessary to the health of the king, resolved to make it agreeable to herself too, and gave the first orders for enlarging the gardens.'

The team charged with realizing William and Mary's vision was led by Hans Willem Bentinck, 1st Earl of Portland, the King's childhood friend and trusted adviser, who had supervised the new gardens at Het Loo. He appointed a number of fellow Dutchmen to serve under his direction, but chose an Englishman, George London, as his deputy. Together with his apprentice Henry Wise, London had undertaken a host of highly successful gardens projects, including work at Burghley House, Chatsworth House and Dyrham Park (fig. 32).

At first, London was obliged to limit his activities to the laying out of paths and walks, so as not to interrupt the works to the house itself. But he subsequently made rapid progress, creating a magnificent parterre garden in front of the King's Apartments. This was composed of eight square or rectangular divisions, with a wide, tree-lined walk – today called Dial Walk – running down the middle. Each division was laid out in intricate geometric patterns of turf and flower beds, bordered with low hedges and dwarf trees. The strict formality of the gardens was offset by a feature that lay to the east of the palace and was intended more for entertainment: a bowling green.

In front of the Queen's Apartments there was a 'Little Flower Garden', which was reached by a small bridge and a staircase that led out from the first floor of the apartments. To the west was a fine avenue lined with eighty large elm trees that ran all the way from the palace to the Hammersmith Road, forming a clear boundary with Hyde Park. The large tract of land to the north of the palace was left untouched for now, although an area was fenced off as an enclosure for asses. It is possible that this was to provide milk for the Queen's baths, as was fashionable for rich ladies. She and William also laid out considerable sums on the creation of gravel walks and borders, and the vast number and variety of trees and plants used throughout reflect their Dutch tastes in garden design.

33. The deathbed of Mary II, 1694. The details of the room are probably fanciful, but the large number of attendants is accurate. The Queen's doctors are shown on the extreme left, and the Archbishop of Canterbury sits opposite them. The King himself can be seen coming into the room.

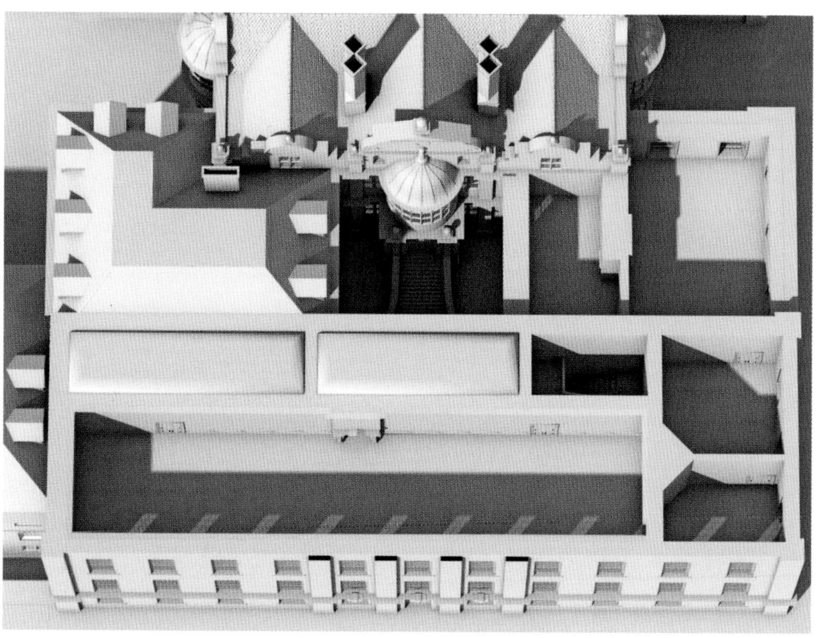

34. (above) Reconstructed view of Kensington Palace as it might have looked in 1690–95, with new pavilions added to the original Jacobean house.

35. (left) Cutaway reconstruction showing the King's Gallery range, built across the south fronts of the two southern pavilions in 1695. In the courtyard behind, the original Jacobean house can still be seen.

The King and Queen continued to live at Kensington while the works to the garden and palace were being completed, enjoying some much-needed domestic peace and stability. But it would prove all too brief. On the morning of 21 December 1694, Mary woke feeling unwell. She noticed a rash on her arms and soon realized that it was smallpox, one of the most feared and virulent diseases of the age. With admirable calm, she put her papers in order, wrote instructions for her funeral and took an inventory of her jewels. By contrast, her husband was greatly distressed. Although they had married for dynastic reasons, they had come to love each other deeply, and William had once declared that during the whole course of their marriage, he had 'never known one single fault in her'. On receiving the news of his wife's illness, the King was heard to remark that 'from being the happiest', he was now going to be 'the miserablest creature on earth'.

Caring little for the risk of infection, William stayed by Mary's side throughout the desperate days of her illness, and slept on a camp bed in her room (fig. 33). When she breathed her last on 28 December, he was

36. Kensington Palace from the south-east, showing the King's Gallery range (left) added to the palace in 1695.

37. (left) The exterior of William III's new gallery was embellished with a lion's head cornice carved by William Emmett and painted to imitate stone.

38. *(below)* Charles I and Henrietta Maria with Their Two Eldest Children, Prince Charles and Princess Mary *by Sir Anthony van Dyck, 1631–32. This painting was hung in the King's Gallery during the reign of William III.*

so grief-stricken that many believed he would soon follow her to the grave. Her lead-lined coffin caused some damage to the Queen's stairs as it was carried down them for burial at Westminster Abbey, and the account books include a payment to one John Churchill for their repair.

The immediate impact of Mary's death was William's abandonment of the building work at Hampton Court, in which she had taken a keen interest. A chronic shortage of funds also prompted his decision to leave the great rooms empty and unfurnished, and it was not until Whitehall Palace burnt down in 1698 that he was obliged to resurrect the works.

In the meantime, the King concentrated his efforts on Kensington, where he was now spending most of his time. In the spring of 1695, he embarked on the last major addition to the palace until the 1720s: the King's Gallery range (figs. 36 and 37). This extended across the south of the house, concealing the two southern pavilions and enclosing the space between them (now known as White Court; figs. 34 and 35).

The main room of the new wing was an extensive gallery, eleven windows across and built of brick. Rather plain and unprepossessing from the outside, the interior housed some seventy-one pictures chosen by

the King. These comprised some of the very best paintings from the royal collection, including seven Titians, two Michelangelos, a Leonardo and the famous portrait of Charles I and his family by Sir Anthony van Dyck (fig. 38). Over the fireplace, William installed a wind-dial, or 'anemoscope', made by the clockmaker Robert Norden with painted scenes of the four continents (Australia was not discovered until the later eighteenth century; fig. 39).

After the completion of the gallery, the Great Stair was replaced by a lavish new staircase crafted from stone on a significantly larger scale. These new additions, which were completed in 1696, gave Kensington a stateliness that had previously been lacking. With the exception of a few minor repairs during the remainder of William's reign, the building works had finally come to a close (fig. 40). It had taken six years to transform the original house into a palace, add new refinements and deal with unexpected misfortunes. Kensington had therefore been the product of evolution rather than a single, unified design. Its external simplicity formed a marked contrast to the lavish internal decorations, which lent it the magnificence required of a royal residence – albeit one modest in scale compared to Hampton Court.

The celebrated writer and diarist John Evelyn had described Kensington as 'yet a patch'd building' in its early days, but by the end of William's reign he acknowledged that it was 'very noble, tho' not great'. Rather more complimentary was the anonymous author of *The New Description and State of England,* who in 1701 enthused that Kensington was 'a magnificent palace ... now one of the most sumptuous palaces of the royal family'.

In February 1702, William suffered a fall while riding in Hampton Court or Bushy Park, when his horse stumbled on a molehill. He landed awkwardly on his right shoulder and broke his collarbone.

39. The 'anemoscope', or wind-dial, above the fireplace in the King's Gallery. The most important feature of the interior to survive from William's time, it was linked to a vane on the palace roof, and the hand indicated the direction from which the wind was blowing.

That evening, he travelled by carriage to Kensington, where the fracture was reset. Although he spent the next few days convalescing, in early March he was struck down by a fever and respiratory problems. By 6 March he was well enough to take a little exercise in the King's Gallery, but the exertion proved too much and he fell asleep on a chair near an open window and caught a chill. He died in his 'new little Bedchamber' two days later, surrounded by courtiers and favourites.

40. This painting of fallow deer in the royal paddock at Kensington, attributed to Francis Barlow, c. 1695, is the earliest known view of William III's newly completed palace.

Kensington under Queen Anne, 1702–14

William III's successor was his sister-in-law, Anne, who received the momentous news of her accession while staying at St James's Palace, where she had lived with her father, James II, when he was Duke of York. Due to an extraordinary, tragic quirk of fate, she would be the last monarch of the Stuart dynasty to rule Britain.

By the time of her accession, Anne had been pregnant no fewer than seventeen times. Only five children had been born alive, all of whom had died in infancy or childhood. Anne's son William, Duke of Gloucester, had been her greatest hope, and had been greatly adored by his uncle and aunt, William and Mary, who were themselves childless (fig. 41). The young Duke had often stayed at Kensington, and there is a charming account of his playing soldiers at the age of five with some companions outside the palace, where they were formally reviewed by King William. But he had always been a sickly child and he died in 1700, shortly after his eleventh birthday. His uncle was grief-stricken and told the boy's mother, 'It is so great a loss to me as well as to all England, that it pierces my heart with affliction.'

Although William had refused Anne's request to visit him at Kensington at the end of his life, her accession was never in doubt. One of the King's last acts was to approve the formal barring of the claim of the 'Old Pretender', James Francis Edward Stuart, son of James II. William, who had found his formal duties increasingly burdensome after Mary's death, had also called on Anne to host a number of court functions at Kensington in recent years, such as the card games that were described by a local newspaper in November 1699:

> Upon Monday last there was a great appearance at Kensington; but that which most graced it was, That Her Royal Highness the Princess of Denmark [Anne], with a train of above sixty ladies of the first quality in town, made up that glorious circle. The place of this noble appearance was in the great gallery at the Royal Palace at Kensington, a room both for largeness, and rich furniture, suited as it were for such a reception: There were in it two large basset tables, at one of which his most gracious Majesty, with Their Royal Highnesses the Princess and Prince of Denmark, entertained themselves at play, whilst many other smaller tables on each side of the room were filled with persons of the best qualities.

There had been another purpose to such gatherings, however. William was all too well aware of his waning popularity after Mary's death. His naturally xenophobic English subjects had tolerated him as

41. Queen Anne with her son, William, Duke of Gloucester, from the studio of Sir Godfrey Kneller, c. 1694. William III doted on his young nephew and astonished courtiers by joining in the child's games. The boy's death in 1700 led to the eventual succession of George I.

42. Table plan for the Queen's Dinner, 6 February 1704, from Royal Cookery; or, The Complete Court-Cook, *1710, by Patrick Lamb, who joined the Royal Household in 1660 and served as 1st Master Cook between 1689 and 1709.*

the husband of a home-grown queen, but as a sole monarch he was a good deal less acceptable. He had therefore increasingly placed Anne centre stage, relying on her popularity as a princess of Stuart blood.

Nevertheless, relations between William and his sister-in-law had not always been easy. The King had no liking for Anne's husband, Prince George of Denmark. Neither did he approve of her devotion to her confidante, Sarah Churchill, Duchess of Marlborough. Sarah was a shrewd political operator, and although her husband was William's most distinguished soldier, he was also an unfaithful political supporter and was often in disgrace.

Anne was thirty-seven at the time of her accession. Her numerous pregnancies had taken their toll on her figure, contributing to the gout that plagued her from her mid-thirties and left her barely able to walk. But the new Queen made up for her physical deficiencies with the power of her personality. She had inherited the charm of her late uncle Charles II, and had the popular touch that William had so markedly lacked. Charles had arranged voice training for his niece, and when she gave her first speech to Parliament as Queen, she won widespread acclaim for declaring, 'I know my heart to be entirely English.' After more than seven years of being ruled by a widowed Dutchman, it was exactly what her people wanted to hear.

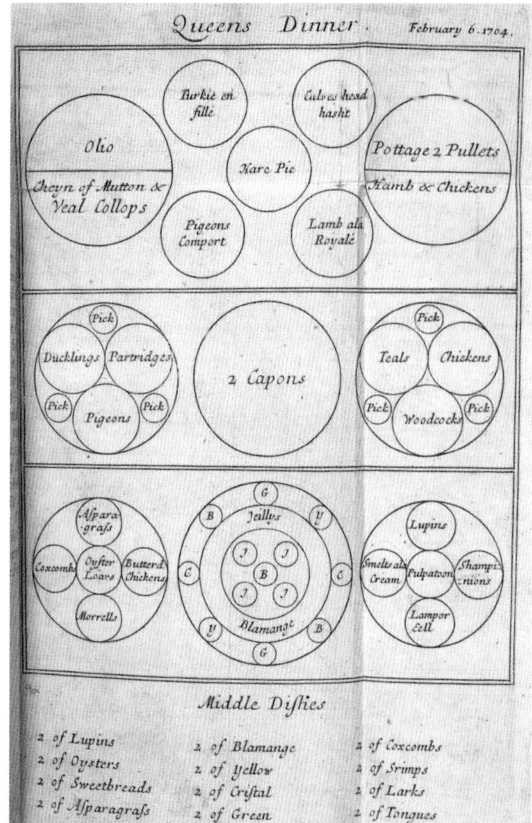

Anne also displayed the perfect blend of high regard for the ancient ceremonies and pageantry of the Crown and firm commitment to a modernized monarchy. During her reign, the notion of a constitutional monarchy, in which the sovereign reigned and the ministers ruled, was consolidated, thereby laying the foundations for the modern state of Britain.

For the first few years of her reign, Anne spent little time at Kensington, preferring the familiarity and convenience of St James's. She did, though, hold audiences and dinners there so frequently that she required a permanent kitchen staff (fig. 42). But the Queen rarely stayed the night at the palace, and she and her husband used it primarily as a winter residence – as her sister, Mary, had originally intended. From 1705, however, Anne began to

43. Pier table with marble top inlaid with Queen Anne's cipher, attributed to Thomas Pelletier, c. 1703–1704. This magnificent table was made for the Queen, probably to stand in the King's Gallery.

pay Kensington more attention, perhaps encouraged by the benefits of its clean air to her husband, who, like William, suffered from asthma.

Anne made a number of modest improvements to the palace (fig. 43). As a queen regnant, she occupied the King's Apartments, while her husband took up residence in the Queen's, which were redecorated to his tastes. They were known as the 'Denmark Wing' until well into the twentieth century. Meanwhile, Anne's occupation of the King's Apartments necessitated some practical changes. In 1706 she commissioned a new dressing room and closet near to the bedchamber, and also planned a new drawing room, although the latter was abandoned by this thrifty monarch in favour of refurnishing an existing room. These rooms were necessary because, as a female sovereign, she was unable to hold formal *levées* and *couchées* as King William had done.

As well as occupying the Queen's Apartments, Prince George was given part of the lodgings that had belonged to William III's favourite, the Earl of Albemarle. These had the advantage of easier

44. Playing card of about 1711, showing Queen Anne (seated) bestowing the office of Groom of the Stool on Elizabeth Seymour, Duchess of Somerset. This prestigious office had previously been held by Sarah Churchill, Duchess of Marlborough, with whom the Queen had finally fallen out in the previous year.

communication with his wife's rooms, which in turn afforded the couple a greater degree of intimate domesticity than was usual for the reigning monarch.

Foremost among the Queen's bedchamber ladies was Sarah Churchill, who was promoted to Groom of the Stool on Anne's accession. By now, she reigned supreme over the rest of the household – and even the Queen herself. Losing her mother at the age of six and being separated from her father had made Anne reserved and lonely. She had subsequently forged a number of close friendships with women, and by far the most significant was with Sarah. In addition to promoting the Duchess to the most sought-after position in her household, the Queen awarded her husband with a plethora of military commands, together with the honour of serving as ambassador extraordinary to the Dutch Republic. She also granted the Duke of Marlborough the royal estate of Woodstock in Oxfordshire and the commission of the future Blenheim Palace, the model design for which was presented by John Vanbrugh to the Queen at Kensington.

The Duke's wife, meanwhile, was assigned generous lodgings at Kensington over two floors, close to the backstairs in Anne's privy lodgings. However, Sarah refused ever to spend the night there, ostensibly on the grounds of comfort. Spying an opportunity, Anne's bedchamber woman, Abigail Masham, an impoverished cousin of the Duchess who was rapidly gaining favour with the Queen, took over part of Sarah's apartment and encouraged her friends to do so, too. When the Duchess found out, she was outraged and demanded that Mrs Masham's belongings be removed.

By now, the Queen and the Duchess were utterly inseparable. 'I cannot live without you', Anne told Sarah on more than one occasion. They referred to each other as 'Mrs Morley' and 'Mrs Freeman' so that the closeness of their friendship would not be disrupted by Anne's new status as Queen. But the Duchess increasingly abused her position in order to further her own interests and those of her family. As Keeper of the Privy Purse, she also kept the Queen hopelessly short of money, and in later years treated her with open contempt.

In thrall though she was to her favourite, Anne eventually reached the limits of her forbearance. In August 1708 the two women had a very public spat when the Duchess told her royal mistress to 'Be quiet' as she stepped out of the royal coach. She had gone too far. Anne never forgave this insult to her majesty and declared that she 'desired nothing but that she [Sarah] would leave off teasing and tormenting' her.

The end came in a dramatic scene in April 1710, when the Duchess – who by now had been supplanted in the Queen's affections by Abigail Masham (with whom Sarah claimed Anne was having a lesbian affair) – pursued the Queen to Kensington, where she confronted her in one of her closets and received a sharp rebuttal. They never saw each other again. In the following year, Anne dismissed the Duchess and her husband from all their offices (fig. 44).

Three years earlier, Anne had lost her beloved husband, George (fig. 45). The couple had spent rather more time at Kensington after their improvements to the palace, including a prolonged spell from September 1707 until June 1708. By now, Prince George was seriously disabled by gout and asthma, and seems to have been confined to rooms on the ground floor. In 1707 a 'new library' had been created for him, for which Grinling Gibbons had been commissioned to provide carvings. The royal couple had returned to Kensington in September

45. Prince George of Denmark by John Riley, 1687–88? After the Prince's death at Kensington on 28 October 1708, his body remained in the palace until 13 November, when it was removed for burial in Westminster Abbey.

46. Johannes Kip after Leonard Knyff's view of 1707 of Kensington Palace and gardens from the south. This is the earliest known view of William and Mary's great parterre garden, probably as it was altered for Queen Anne.

oyal Palace at Kensington

1708, but it had been their last stay together; Prince George died at the palace on 28 October.

Anne felt the loss of her husband keenly. Theirs had been a happy marriage, marked by mutual love and affection. But it had failed in the one thing that mattered for royal alliances: it had produced no surviving heirs to continue their dynasty. Increasingly, Anne was beset by the need to settle the succession. Her closest blood relative was the 'Old Pretender', but his refusal to relinquish his Catholicism negated his claim. Among the many potential Protestant successors, King William's preference had been for Sophia, Dowager Electress of Hanover, partly because her north German state would have made a useful ally for the Dutch against the French. Sophia was the granddaughter of James I (1603–25), and although she had openly supported the claim of James II's son, the 'Old Pretender', her own son George had persuaded her to look more favourably on the idea of inheriting the English throne herself.

Anne left Kensington after her husband's death and stayed away for eighteen months. On her return to the palace, she made several further improvements. All, though, were dictated by the need for economy because the monarchy now drew its income from the new Civil List, which was controlled by the government. Anne's necessary thriftiness is reflected in the fact that William III's crimson, orange and blue private bed was brought from Hampton Court and remade into a new state bed. It survived Anne's entire reign and probably became the bed in which she died (fig. 47).

The Queen did, however, invest significant sums in improving the gardens at Kensington. These had fallen into a state of neglect after her sister Mary's death, and in May 1702 Anne had written to the Duchess of Marlborough, 'I went to Kensington to walk in the garden, which would be a very pretty place if it were well kept, but nothing can be worse.' She soon appointed George London's former apprentice Henry Wise to lead the garden team, and he wasted no time in setting in train a major programme of works to repair, update and extend the gardens.

The paths of the southern parterre were improved with new gravel, while the sand that had defined some of the more delicate *allées* was replaced with cockleshells. New turf cut in Hyde Park and Blackheath was used to restore the grassy walks and replace some of the box-tree hedges, which Anne disliked. The parterre was enlivened with a series of fountains, and an alcove seat designed by Sir Christopher Wren was installed at the southern end of Dial Walk (fig. 46). This was

47. The bed in which Queen Anne reputedly died at Kensington in 1714, now on display at Warwick Castle. It was constructed out of William III's bed.

later moved to the north-eastern corner of the gardens, close to the Bayswater Road, and remains there in its original form today.

In 1704 Wise embarked on work to develop a new wilderness garden to the north of the palace. It would eventually occupy nearly 30 acres, taking back land managed by the Housekeeper. It was planted with three thickly wooded plantations, cut through with stately avenues and winding walkways, and also included an ingenious sunken garden. Wise's creation won widespread acclaim among contemporaries. The writer and politician Joseph Addison enthused, 'It must have been a fine genius for gardening, that could have thought of forming such an unsightly hollow into so beautiful an area, and to have hit the eye with so uncommon and agreeable a scene as that which is now wrought.'

Increasingly, the gardens at Kensington became a source of delight not just for the Queen but also for the people of London. Access was gained through a series of new gates. The formal gardens around the palace could be visited when the court was not in residence, for a fee paid to the gatekeeper. Entrance was through the avenue leading off the Hammersmith Road, and a second entry led off Kensington Church Street, via the kitchen garden. Once the new wilderness had been completed, a new gate was installed so that visitors could approach this part of the garden from the Acton Road, on the northern side of the site. Many visitors were prompted by curiosity; the

fashionable, in their high heels, came to be seen; and others came to appreciate the wholesome fresh air, peacefulness and beauty. Benches, seats and alcoves were provided, some carved with dolphins and scallop shells, making it an agreeable place for conversation as well as relaxation.

> Where Kensington, high o'er the neighbouring lands
> Midst greens and sweets, a regal fabric, stands,
> And sees each spring, luxuriant in her bowers,
> A snow of blossoms, and a wild of flowers,
> The dames of Britain oft in crowds repair
> To gravel walks, and unpolluted air.
> Here, while the town in damps and darkness lies,
> They breathe in sun-shine, and see azure skies ...

48. The 'greenhouse' or 'Banqueting House', now known as the Orangery, built in 1704–1705 to house delicate plants during the winter and for summer entertainments. It was probably designed by John Vanbrugh, working with Nicholas Hawksmoor. View by Henry Parke, a student of Sir John Soane's office from 1814 to 1820.

Thomas Tickell, who penned this verse, was one of thousands of visitors who soon crowded to the gardens. By 1712 they had become so popular that a set of new instructions was issued to the gatekeepers. They were given permission to eject any visitor who entered the park carrying alcohol. There was to be no jumping off walls or fences and no climbing. All commercial traffic – hackney carriages, coaches and carts – was strictly prohibited.

In the same year that Wise started work on the wilderness garden, Queen Anne approved an estimate for a new greenhouse in which to overwinter the exotic plants and citrus trees that ornamented the gardens during the summer months. Before work began, however, she was persuaded to accept proposals for a more ambitious building, eventually costing twice as much. Begun in September 1704 and completed by December 1705, the resulting structure is architecturally the most accomplished building at Kensington (fig. 48).

The Orangery may have been the work of the celebrated eighteenth-century architects John Vanbrugh and Nicholas Hawksmoor. Vanbrugh was deputy to the Surveyor-General, Sir Christopher Wren, while Hawksmoor was resident Clerk of Works. The interior of the building, which was equipped with

49. The investiture of a Knight of the Garter at Kensington Palace in August 1713, as depicted by Peter Angelis, c. 1725. The ceremony was usually held at Windsor, but Queen Anne was too ill to travel on this occasion.

underfloor heating, contained a vast central space with a coved ceiling and, at either end, domed circular compartments lined with Corinthian columns, with carved detail by Grinling Gibbons.

So magnificent was the new greenhouse that when it was not filled with plants, the Queen made use of it as a banqueting house and to hold the religious ceremony of Touching for the Queen's Evil, to cure the disease known as scrofula. William III had abandoned this ceremony, much to the disgust of his subjects, so Anne's revival signalled her desire both to have more dealings with her subjects and to reinforce the divine nature of royal rule.

More often, however, Anne used Kensington to host small-scale private audiences and investitures, as well as essential cabinet

50. Canopy of state, made by craftsmen of the Great Wardrobe, 1709. This rare example, made for Queen Anne's ambassador to The Hague, has recently been acquired and conserved by Historic Royal Palaces, and is now on display in Kensington Palace.

meetings, especially after her husband's death in 1708 (figs. 49 and 50). The Queen also continued to use Kensington as a winter retreat, and her failing health prompted her to stay here until late spring each year. Her loyal physician, John Arbuthnot, was furnished with a smartly appointed apartment for his constant attendance. The Queen's own private lodgings appear to have received renewed attention, too, as a number of cabinet pictures were moved there from storage or reframed at this time, revealing her personal interest in her art collection. Even in her very last days she requested a meeting with Wren to look at further improvements to the palace, but this was not to be.

Although the Queen's physical (and sometimes mental) health rapidly declined, including debilitating strokes late in 1713, she diligently attended cabinet and council meetings. Acutely conscious that political and religious divisions threatened the peace of her kingdom, to the very last she tried to reassure her new successor, George Louis, Elector of Hanover (George's mother, Sophia, having died in June 1714), of her loyalty to the succession.

On 30 July 1714, Anne had her hair dressed, but then suffered a violent stroke as her ladies and doctors looked on helplessly. She died two days later, aged just forty-nine. To mark her passing, the State Apartments were hung with black cloth and the Great Bedchamber was decked in purple, with a state canopy of the same material for the Queen's body to lie under.

In defiance of the Queen's wishes, her ministers secretly offered the Crown to James II's son on condition that he renounce the Catholic faith. He refused, and the Crown passed peacefully to the Elector of Hanover, now George I. That evening, barrels of strong beer were sent to Kensington Palace and bonfires were lit to toast the accession of the first Hanoverian King of Britain.

Kensington in the Reign of George I, 1714–27

There was no great period of mourning for Queen Anne, such as she had arranged after her husband's death. Even her favoured Groom of the Stool, the Duchess of Somerset, was only too ready to exchange the personal perquisites of her late mistress's deathbed and a pair of earrings for £3000 in cash. It was a sorry end to a dynasty that had ruled Britain for more than a century.

When the messenger arrived at the Palace of Herrenhausen in Hanover with news of Anne's death, the Elector was in bed asleep. It being a dispatch of such importance, permission was granted to wake him. On hearing that he was now King of Great Britain and Ireland, George Louis merely grunted, turned over and went back to sleep (fig. 51). His snores were soon heard reverberating along the corridors of the palace.

The reaction in England was equally muted. The expectation of a Jacobite uprising came to nothing, and the succession of the Hanoverian King was remarkably peaceful: 'Not a mouse stirred against him in England, in Ireland or in Scotland.' In part this was due to the efforts of the Privy Council, which met on 1 August 1714 to establish a regency council to govern until the arrival of the new King.

But George seemed in no hurry to take possession of his kingdom. His interests did not extend far beyond the borders of his beloved Hanover, and he had always disliked the English, with their liberal and upstart ways. 'His views and affections were singly confined to the narrow compass of his Electorate', sneered the courtier Lord Chesterfield. 'England was too big for him.' Certainly, in terms of size alone, George I's new kingdom dwarfed his native lands. In 1714 Britain's population stood at around 5.5 million, while Hanover's was less than one-tenth of that.

There were more fundamental differences, too. In Hanover, the Elector reigned supreme over a population grown accustomed to obedience and discipline. All expenditure over £13 had to receive his personal sanction, and the army was regarded as his private property. His new kingdom, meanwhile, was now established on a constitutional model of government, and the power of the monarch was significantly limited. He was unable to levy new taxes, abolish privileges or make new laws without Parliament's consent. Neither could he order the imprisonment or execution of any subject, or confiscate their lands or property. The last monarch to undermine these liberties had been executed.

When George and his entourage at last crossed the Channel, they were tossed about on rough seas and then detained off Gravesend for several hours by thick fog. The very elements surrounding his new

51. George I in his coronation robes, from the studio of Sir Godfrey Kneller, 1714–25.

52. *Sophia Charlotte von Kielmansegg, Countess of Darlington, the half-sister (and, it was rumoured, mistress) of George I. From the school of Sir Godfrey Kneller*, c. 1714–25.

kingdom seemed as inhospitable as the people within to George, who must have heartily wished himself back in Hanover. Finally, on the evening of 18 September, the royal yacht arrived in Greenwich. It was greeted by the firing of cannons, the ringing of bells and the flying of flags, and the citizens of London thronged the riverside to catch a first glimpse of their new King. A large number of ministers, courtiers and churchmen were among the delegation appointed to greet him. But George's patience had been tested by the tiresome journey and he dismissed them all with scant ceremony before hastening to bed. It was an inauspicious beginning to the new dynasty.

That the new King intended to surround himself with German attendants was obvious from the beginning. His entourage comprised more than seventy-five German servants and courtiers, as well as his two Turkish Grooms of the Chamber, Mehemet and Mustapha (see fig. 2). He was also accompanied by his corpulent half-sister (and, it was rumoured, his mistress), Madame von Kielmansegg, and the emaciated Ehrengard Melusine von der Schulenburg, who was certainly his mistress (fig. 52). It did not take George's new subjects long to nickname them 'the Elephant and the Maypole'.

Notably absent from the King's entourage was his former wife, Sophia Dorothea of Celle (fig. 53). She was in disgrace after having an affair with a Swedish colonel, Philip von Königsmarck, who had subsequently been murdered. George had divorced her and kept her a virtual prisoner in the north German castle of Ahlden, where she remained until her death in 1726. Their children, George Augustus (the future George II) and Sophia Dorothea, were forbidden to see her.

George I settled at St James's Palace, the official seat of the monarchy after the fire that had destroyed Whitehall in 1698. He was soon besieged by a host of courtiers, eager to secure patronage and favour from a new sovereign and a new government. A few of these had visited or even worked in the Elector's court in Hanover during the closing years of Anne's reign, but most Englishmen had little knowledge of their new King. More worrying for George was the prevalence of Jacobites – supporters of James II's son, James Francis Edward Stuart – who were openly hostile. Some of his subjects viewed him with suspicion as another foreign king, while to others he was a 'turnip head', a mere rustic farmer interested only in the fortunes of his native Hanover.

The new King did little to endear himself to his subjects. Naturally shy, he eschewed many of the traditional ceremonies and pageantry that had been upheld by the British monarchy for centuries.

Although he was fluent in French and competent in Italian, he spoke little English and made no effort to improve. He lacked intellectual interests, and the absence of a queen meant that his court lacked the glamour and society offered by the likes of Charles II. Instead, it was dominated by the increasingly acrimonious relations between the King and his son, George, Prince of Wales, who capitalized on his father's unpopularity and began to gather a rival court about him.

George I had inspected Kensington shortly after his arrival and liked it 'very well', seeing little immediate need to improve upon it. But neither did he see anything to tempt him to reside there. Instead, he remained at St James's, putting up with its rather cramped conditions because of the convenience that it offered for parliamentary and other government business. He soon had cause to think again, however, because the palace was rapidly being engulfed by London's westward expansion. This had not yet reached Kensington, which still enjoyed the clean air and tranquillity of its rural situation. The new King therefore began to pay it more favourable attention.

In 1716 George I commissioned some urgent repair works at Kensington. In June of that year, an official report noted that the 'Old Front' was 'much cracked and out of repair, especially the Bow Window' – a reference to the north wall of the former Nottingham House. In the following month, orders were given 'to take down the front wall, roof and floors of the Privy Chamber', which was lit by this window, 'and to rebuild the same in a plain and substantial manner'. But this was just the tip of the iceberg. A survey of December 1717 concluded that the 'old body of the house' – weakened, presumably, by endless alterations and perhaps constructed none too solidly in the first place – would have to be completely rebuilt.

Sir Christopher Wren was once more commissioned to draw up a series of ambitious plans for the remodelling of Kensington Palace. The first proposed the complete replacement of Nottingham House by a new block containing two large rooms at State Apartment level. The second, more modest plan retained part of the old house, but envisaged a vast westward extension of the King's Gallery range and the creation of new rooms and a formal façade to the east. Sir John Vanbrugh, meanwhile, submitted typically ambitious plans for a vast new

53. Sophia Dorothea of Celle, wife of George I (then Electoral Prince of Hanover), with their two children, Sophia Dorothea and George Augustus (later George II), in a portrait by Jacques Vaillant, c. 1690. Her affair with the Swedish courtier Philip von Königsmarck led to banishment for life in a remote German castle.

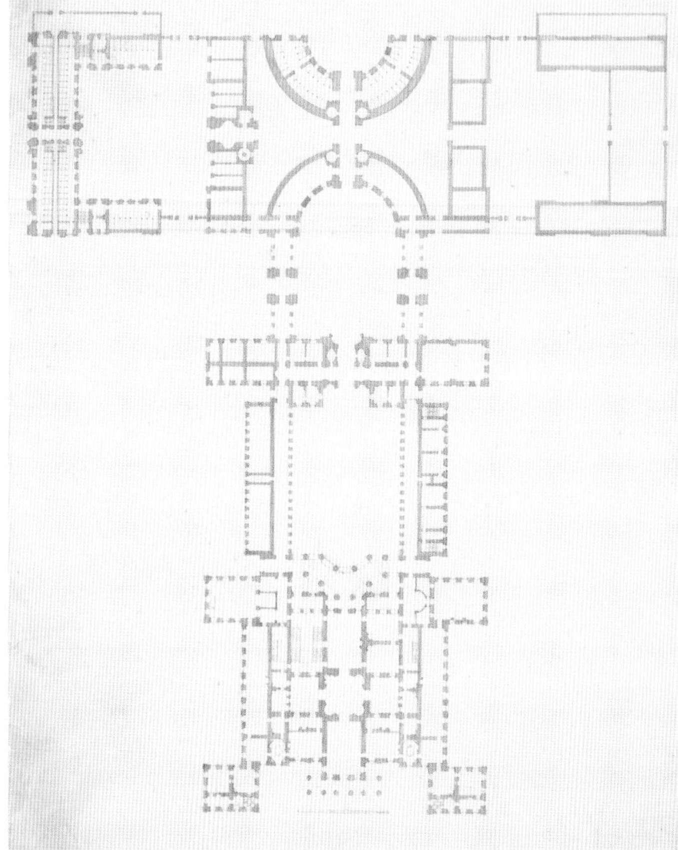

54. The scheme submitted by Sir John Vanbrugh in 1718 for a palatial rebuilding of Kensington Palace. If it had gone ahead, only the King's Gallery (lower left) would have survived from the original building.

baroque complex, similar in scale to Blenheim Palace. But this was his own idea rather than the King's, and it was swiftly rejected (fig. 54).

In the end, Wren's scheme was also turned down in favour of a pioneering design of the 'Palladian' school that was to dominate English architecture for the next generation. This shift in architectural style was due as much to politics as to taste. The Whigs were now in the ascendancy, thanks to their support for the Hanoverian succession. The ideas and tastes of the Tories, meanwhile, were closely associated with the Stuart dynasty and were now roundly rejected. These were encapsulated by the English version of the baroque style developed by Wren, Hawksmoor and Vanbrugh.

In place of this ostentatious style were the simpler, more elegant designs developed in the sixteenth century by the Italian Andrea

55. The East Front of Kensington Palace, with Part of the Great Lawn *by John Tinney after Anthony Highmore, 1744. The tall block in the centre of the building was added in 1718–21.*

56. (left) George I's state bed from Kensington, 1723. The bed, which is now at Chatsworth House, has the only remains of the original silk damask hung at Kensington from this period.

57. (below) William Kent by William Aikman, c. 1723–25. *As well as being one of the most popular architects of the Georgian age, Kent was a bon viveur with a wide circle of friends among the artists and writers of the day.*

Palladio and inspired by Roman architecture. The leading architect of the Palladian style in England was Colen Campbell, aided by the patronage of the so-called 'Architect Earl', Richard Boyle, 3rd Earl of Burlington. It was probably Campbell who was responsible for the new work that George I commissioned at Kensington, although this was in theory directed by William Benson, who replaced the eighty-five-year-old Wren as Surveyor-General in May 1718.

Undeterred by the adverse reports about the state of the existing building, the King and his court had taken up residence at Kensington in April 1718 and stayed there until early August. Not long after their departure, work on Campbell's scheme began in earnest, and the shell of the new building was probably complete by the end of 1719 (fig. 55). The three most important rooms were the King's Drawing Room, which overlooked the park, the Cupola Room (as it became known) in the centre, and the Privy Chamber to the west.

In the meantime, Benson had been dismissed as Surveyor-General after just over a year in the post. He was replaced by Sir Thomas Hewett, a man of similar background and architectural tastes, but a less objectionable nature. In early 1720 King George ordered Hewett to

58. *(below) The Cupola Room, showing William Kent's painted decoration of the walls, completed in 1725. The chandeliers are modern but evoke the design of the lost originals, probably devised by Kent and made by the London firm of Gumley and Moore.*

59. *(below, right) The ceiling of the Cupola Room, painted by William Kent in 1722. The appointment of the little-known Kent sparked controversy, but his brilliance led to further commissions at Kensington in the years that followed.*

fit out the interiors of the new rooms. He stipulated that the two lower floors were to be completed in the 'cheapest and plainest manner', but approved plans to spend more than twice the cost of the other two for the 'upper and best storey', or State Apartments.

George I's greatest legacy at Kensington is the painted decoration that he commissioned. This was carried out between 1722 and 1727 by a relatively unknown painter and architect with no official position: William Kent (fig. 57). It proved a brilliant if controversial appointment – for Kensington as well as Kent, propelling him to the status of one of the most prolific and successful Palladian designers of the age.

Kent's masterpiece was the Cupola Room ceiling (fig. 59). This was an architectural *trompe l'œil*, representing a four-sided coffered cupola of a type often found in classical Roman buildings, but with a Garter Star at its apex – intended, perhaps, to emphasize the 'Britishness' of the

60. The Queen's Eating Room by Thomas Sutherland after James Stephanoff, from W.H. Pyne's History of the Royal Residences, *1819. The table to the left, composed of a marble top supported by carved and gilded sphinxes, was probably one of a set designed by William Kent for the Cupola Room.*

61. The Privy Chamber by Thomas Sutherland after Charles Wild, from W.H. Pyne's History of the Royal Residences, *1819. This early view shows William Kent's painted ceiling, two of his sculptural tables and remnants of George I's picture hang.*

62. (opposite) William Kent's preparatory drawing for the ceiling of the King's Drawing Room, 1722.

63. (left) The ceiling of the King's Drawing Room, painted in 1722–23. The subject is the destruction of the nymph Semele, mother of Bacchus, by her lover Jupiter.

64. Detail from the ceiling of the Presence Chamber, for which William Kent was paid in 1724. The central roundel shows the sun god, Apollo, in his chariot.

65. The King's Gallery, restored to its appearance in George I's reign, with Camillo Rusconi's sculptures of the Four Seasons on pedestals by the windows.

Hanoverian dynasty. The illusion created by the painting was enhanced by the real form of the ceiling, which has steeply curved or coved sides. Kent later painted the walls, decorating them with more *trompe l'œil* detailing to the existing pilasters, with swags and military trophies between them. He probably also designed the eighteen stools and four large chandeliers that adorn the room (figs. 58 and 60).

The result was a dazzling success that cannot have failed to impress the King. Certainly, he did not hesitate to set Kent to work on the two other new rooms and seven further spaces in the palace. The architect began in 1722–23 with the King's Drawing Room, where he filled the ceiling oval with a mythological scene showing Jupiter and his lover Semele (figs. 62 and 63). In 1723 he also completed the ceiling of the Privy Chamber with a representation of Mars and Minerva, the god of war and the goddess of wisdom; they may have been intended to represent the Prince and Princess of Wales (fig. 61). In October he moved on to the King's Bedchamber, where he decorated the ceiling in the 'grotesque' style. This has since been destroyed, but a similar example can be found in the Presence Chamber, with a central roundel showing the sun god, Apollo, in his chariot (fig. 64).

Kent's most ambitious project at Kensington was the King's Gallery, which he began in 1725. He replaced most of Wren's interior with his own design, which included painting the woodwork in white and gold, with red damask covering the walls (fig. 65). This made the gallery one of the first examples in England of the white, gold and red formula that would remain fashionable for the rest of the eighteenth century. The most striking feature, however, was the ceiling, which Kent adorned with a series of seven scenes in oil on canvas from the *Odyssey* (fig. 66). These were linked and surrounded by an elaborate architectural *trompe l'œil*. The picture hang included two large Van Dyck portraits of Charles I and the royal family – further reminders of George I's ancestry through King Charles's sister.

At the same time, Kent was commissioned to give the newly embellished apartments a suitably impressive introduction by redecorating the Great Stair (now known as the King's Staircase; fig. 67). The windows in the north wall were blocked in order to provide a blank

66. Detail from the ceiling painting in the King's Gallery, completed in 1727. The scene, from the story of Odysseus, shows Mercury arriving at Calypso's house. William Kent probably collaborated with his friend Alexander Pope, who translated Homer's Odyssey.

67. The King's Staircase, created by William Kent between 1725 and 1727. Several recognizable members of George I's court are depicted, pressing up against the trompe l'œil *balustrade.*

68. (left) William Kent could not resist including a portrait of himself in the King's Staircase mural, shown here with his palette and his mistress, looking down from the ceiling at the court below.

69. (below) Peter the Wild Boy (in the green coat) is among the courtiers depicted on the King's Staircase. Beside him stands Dr John Arbuthnot, satirist, medical doctor and Peter's tutor.

surface for painting, and the west wall was rebuilt further out into the courtyard and provided with the existing Venetian window. Kent's decorative scheme was inspired by the Georgian court, and there are several recognizable individuals among the figures – including, on the ceiling, the artist himself, shown wearing a brown turban and holding an artist's palette (fig. 68). The King's Turkish servants, Mehemet and Mustapha, are also featured, as is Peter the Wild Boy, a feral child found in the woods in Germany (figs. 2 and 69).

A number of other building works were commissioned during George I's reign, although most fell into the category of essential repairs rather than embellishments. They included the replacement of the 'mean and decayed' service buildings around what was then called Kitchen Court. The old kitchens were replaced with the existing residential range occupying the western half of the north range to Clock Court. The north side of the new court was occupied by a substantial self-contained house, which was probably designed by Kent and intended for the King's mistress, Ehrengard Melusine von der Schulenburg. From 1729, it was used by Prince Frederick (figs. 70 and 71), since which time the court has been known as the 'Prince of Wales's' (fig. 72).

70. *(above) The main stair of the house forming the north side of the Prince of Wales's Court in the 1720s. From 1729 the house was occupied by Prince Frederick, who became Prince of Wales on the death of his grandfather George I in 1727.*

71. *(below) Frederick, Prince of Wales, by Christian Friedrich Zincke, 1729. Although he was their eldest son and heir, Frederick was despised by George II and Queen Caroline.*

Between the new buildings and the back of the Queen's Gallery range lay Green Cloth Court, named after the Board of Green Cloth, which managed the domestic economy of the Royal Household and whose Kensington office overlooked it. In 1724 open brick arcades were added to the northern side of the courtyard, above which a series of rooms was soon added for the Prince of Wales's daughters – hence its renaming as the Princesses' Court.

Although the gardens at Kensington had received a great deal of attention from his predecessors, George I saw fit to make further improvements once the works to the palace itself were largely complete. Henry Wise had been retained as Master Gardener, but by 1716 his health was deteriorating and he obtained the King's permission to share the burden of the royal gardens contract with his long-standing colleague Joseph Carpenter.

The King's attention was drawn first to the 100-acre paddock between Kensington Gardens and Hyde Park, where his 'first intention ... was that of having animals of different kinds, kept to run and feed at liberty all over the whole'. From the beginning of the reign a number of red deer, elk and horses had wandered freely across the plot, but more exotic species were now introduced, including a tiger, two civets and what were described as 'outlandish birds'. In keeping with an ancient kingly tradition, this effectively created a menagerie such as had been maintained at the Tower of London since the thirteenth century.

All of the improvements that George I made to Kensington and its surrounds inspired him to make more use of the palace. In August 1721, Lady Lechmere, who lived at nearby Campden House, wrote that 'the court is now in our neighbourhood; they say the King is extremely well pleased with his apartments.' Vanbrugh wrote in a similar vein in the following year, telling Lord Carlisle, 'The king is much pleased with Kensington, and the easy way of living he has fallen into there.'

Before long, it was obvious that George intended to make Kensington one of his most frequented houses. In 1723 Vanbrugh confidently predicted that the rental value of his own lodgings at Kensington would rise significantly as a result. ''Tis easy to imagine it may be worth considerably more when the King comes to Spend so much of his time there, as I find 'tis taken for granted he will', he told Henry Joynes, Hawksmoor's replacement as Clerk of Works. Ironically, however, it was the same building work that the King had commissioned that prevented his spending more time at Kensington, 'for want of the new Rooms being ready for the King's use'. Nevertheless, he did stay there

72. The north-eastern corner of the Prince of Wales's Court, as created in the 1720s.

for a total of more than two years during his reign, in addition to the numerous day visits he made to the palace and gardens (fig. 73).

When he did stay at the palace, George used the King's Apartments created by William III. In the absence of a consort, the Queen's Apartments remained empty until they were taken over by his daughter-in-law, Caroline, when she became Queen in 1727. Although she and her husband, the Prince of Wales, would ordinarily have had apartments at the palace, their increasingly hostile relationship with George I meant that they never stayed there. They spent a great deal of time at Hampton Court instead, and after 1718 they settled at Leicester House in central London.

However, the King had wrested control of the couple's three young daughters, Anne, Amelia and Caroline, who all stayed at Kensington when required (fig. 74). He appeared to dote on his granddaughters, and spared no expense for their comfort. In 1720 there was a delivery of three field bedsteads of yellow mohair with 'pieces of mohair lined with paragon ... to prevent the youngest princess from falling out'. The three girls were assigned more than sixty attendants at the palace.

But the King's hostile treatment of the Prince and Princess of Wales was to have tragic consequences. The birth of their son George William in November 1717 prompted a furious row with the King over the choice of godparents at the child's christening. The infant prince was evidently sickly, and the royal physicians advised that he be moved to Kensington

73. (overleaf) Aerial view of Kensington Palace from the south-east. Although the surroundings of the palace have changed considerably since the reign of George I, the general form of the building remains much as he left it.

74. Princesses Anne, Amelia and Caroline by Martin Maingaud, 1721. The three eldest daughters of George II had apartments on the north side of Green Cloth Court, which soon acquired its present name of Princesses' Court.

'for the benefit of the air'. Still furious with his son and daughter-in-law, the King restricted their visits, and the little boy died in February 1718.

The rift between the King and his popular son and daughter-in-law prompted George to make a much greater effort in the life of his court. From April to August 1718 he staged the busiest and most spectacular round of court entertainments that had ever been seen in Kensington's history. There were thrice-weekly 'Drawing Rooms' and also much larger-scale events with music, dancing and fireworks, which made use of the gardens and Orangery as well as the palace. The usually unsociable King had pulled out all the stops, as one participant noted: 'The ladies say they never see so much company and every body fine, the King very obliging and in great good humour ... all the garden illuminated and music and dancing in the Green House and the long Gallery' (fig. 75). Exhausted by the effort, George retreated to Hanover for the next two summers. On his return, he was reconciled to the Prince and subsequently reverted to his reclusive ways.

In the absence of a queen, by far the most prominent female resident at the palace during George I's reign was the King's half-sister, Sophia von Kielmansegg, now Countess of Darlington, with her three daughters (publicly regarded as the King's 'nieces'). The great intellect and socialite Lady Mary Wortley Montagu was one of the few who admired Sophia, and gave her the rather backhanded compliment of having 'greater vivacity in conversation than ever I knew in a German of either sex'. More common were the descriptions of Madame von Kielmansegg's unprepossessing appearance. Robert Walpole's son Horace stayed at Kensington as a boy and remembered being terrified 'at her enormous figure. The fierce black eyes, large and rolling, beneath two lofty arched eyebrows, two acres of cheeks spread with crimson, an ocean of neck that overflowed and was not distinguished from the lower part of her body, and no part restrained by stays.'

The King's mistress, Ehrengard Melusine von der Schulenburg, Duchess of Kendal, also had apartments at Kensington. These overlooked the 'Green Cloth' or Princesses' Court, and an arcaded ground-floor gallery was built there for her convenience in 1724. Lady Mary was rather less polite about this German lady, describing her as 'by no means an inviting object'. She mused that the Duchess's attraction must lay only in the fact that she was 'duller than the King and consequently did not find that he was so'. Be that as it may, the Duchess wielded an enormous amount of influence. The King habitually visited her 'every afternoon between five and eight', which gave her the opportunity to control access to him and act as an intermediary between the monarch and his ministers. One of the most important, Robert Walpole, claimed that the Duchess's position was 'in effect, as much Queen of England as any that ever was', and that 'he did everything by her'.

75. Court dress consisting of an embroidered silk mantua robe and petticoat, probably made in England, 1740–45. These elaborate dresses would have been a common sight at the court gatherings held at Kensington during the reigns of George I and George II.

During his reign, George I reduced the size of the Royal Household, although it still comprised up to 300 individuals when he was in residence at Kensington. The conduct of state business and the routine of court were dictated by the King's natural shyness and dislike of ceremony. He abandoned the traditional *levée* and instead remained in his private apartments until midday, attended only by his Turkish grooms. The King would then emerge and receive official visitors in an adjoining closet, returning to the Bedchamber for dinner, the largest meal of the day, which he ate alone in the mid-afternoon. By contrast, the Prince and Princess of Wales enjoyed all the trappings of ceremony and splendour that royal life had to offer. As Walpole observed, these were 'as pleasing to the son as they were irksome to the father'.

Towards the end of his reign, George I made increasingly frequent returns to his native Electorate, and it was on a journey there in June 1727 that he died suddenly, at the age of sixty-seven. A contemporary report claimed that he had suffered an 'apoplectic fit' after eating an enormous quantity of watermelons.

George II and Queen Caroline, 1727–60

It was a sultry June day in 1727 when Robert Walpole hastened to Richmond Lodge, where the Prince and Princess of Wales were in residence for the summer. As was their custom, they were enjoying an afternoon nap, and it was only after much urging by Walpole that their servants agreed to wake them. Furious at the interruption, the Prince emerged from the royal bedchamber, half-dressed and muttering oaths against the Prime Minister. Walpole promptly lowered his great bulk down on one knee and kissed the Prince's hand, before imparting the momentous news that his father was dead and he was the new King of Great Britain and Ireland. George appeared momentarily perplexed, then enraged, and at last spluttered, 'Dat is von big lie!' before prancing out of the room.

Having collected themselves, the new King and Queen went at once to Leicester House, where they were greeted with the cheers of well-wishers (figs. 76 and 78). The capital's principal royal palace, St James's, was still undergoing improvement works commissioned by George I, so the couple moved to Kensington, taking up residence within two weeks of their accession (fig. 77).

Although they had often been at odds with the late King, George and Caroline had cause to be thankful to him for the substantial improvements that he had made to the palace. Particularly impressive were the lavish state rooms, which provided the perfect setting for court ceremonies and entertainments. One notable occasion was the ball held in 1729 to mark the birthdays of the royal couple's daughters Amelia and Caroline. The eighteen year-old Princess Amelia danced so enthusiastically with the Duke of Grafton, who was almost thirty years her senior, that it sparked rumours of a romance. Music was central to many other court entertainments, and stars from the latest

76. (above) Queen Caroline of Ansbach by Joseph Highmore, c. 1735. The portrait was painted two years before her death, by which time the Queen had grown rather corpulent from drinking too much chocolate.

77. (right) View of Kensington Church Street, c. 1750. The area's expansion from a small village to a substantial town was due largely to the presence of royalty, who made it a fashionable retreat. Given the palace's comparatively modest size, there was also a need for overflow accommodation for courtiers and servants.

78. George II, painted by Robert Edge Pine in 1759, a year before the King's death. He is standing at the top of the King's Staircase at Kensington, and Kent's mural can be seen in the background.

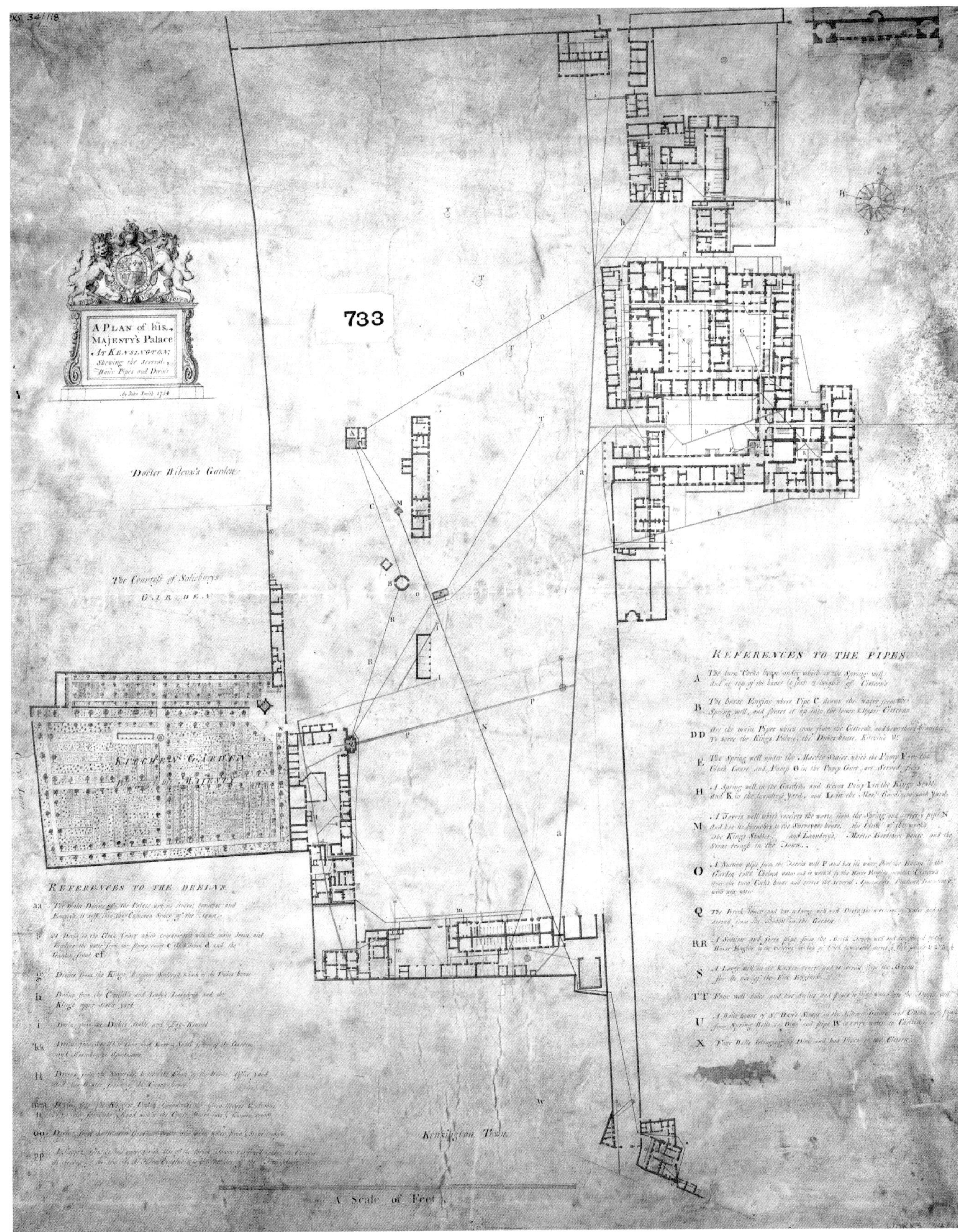

733
A Plan of his Majesty's Palace At Kensington: Shewing the several Water Pipes and Dreins
Docter Wilcox's Garden
The Countess of Salisburys Garden
Kitchen Garden
References to the Pipes
References to the Dreins
Kensington Town
A Scale of Feet

operas and theatre performances flocked to Kensington. George Frideric Handel was among the regular visitors (fig. 80).

Building work to the palace under George II was very limited. Most attention was focused on the gardens, although the palace's service buildings, drainage system and water supply were improved (fig. 79). New furniture was ordered for the State Apartments and for the royal children's rooms in the courtyards to the north-west of the main palace building (fig. 81). Queen Caroline redecorated her gallery (fig. 82) and other rooms, installing a *Wunderkammer* (a collection of curiosities and rarities) in George I's former library and displaying paintings of English monarchs and their consorts throughout the State Apartments. Included in this display was a series of drawings by Hans Holbein the Younger depicting the Tudor royal family and members of their court; the Queen had discovered the long-forgotten works in a bureau in the King's Closet (figs. 83 and 84).

Kensington also offered the rural delights that the royal couple so loved at Richmond, yet within easy reach of Westminster. As soon as they took up residence, the couple set about improving the gardens. Caroline took the lead and commissioned Charles Bridgeman, as Royal Gardener, to remove the beasts from the paddock and send them to the

79. (opposite) Plan of Kensington Palace and its immediate surroundings, 1754. At the top right is the palace itself, together with the stables and coach houses. To the lower left are the kitchen gardens. The largest building in the open space at the centre of the plan is the Foot Guards' barracks of the 1690s.

80. (far left) George Frideric Handel by Thomas Hudson, 1756.

81. (left) William Augustus, Duke of Cumberland, by Charles Jervas, c. 1728. The third and favourite son of George II, the Duke had lodgings at Kensington for most of his life. He is best known as the victor or 'Butcher' of Culloden, the battle of 1746 that brought about the final defeat of the Jacobite Rebellion.

82. *(right)* The Queen's Gallery, Kensington Palace *by Thomas Sutherland after James Stephanoff, from W.H. Pyne's* History of the Royal Residences, *1819. The gallery would have looked much like this in the reign of George II, whose wife, Caroline, had the panelling painted white and arranged the picture hang.*

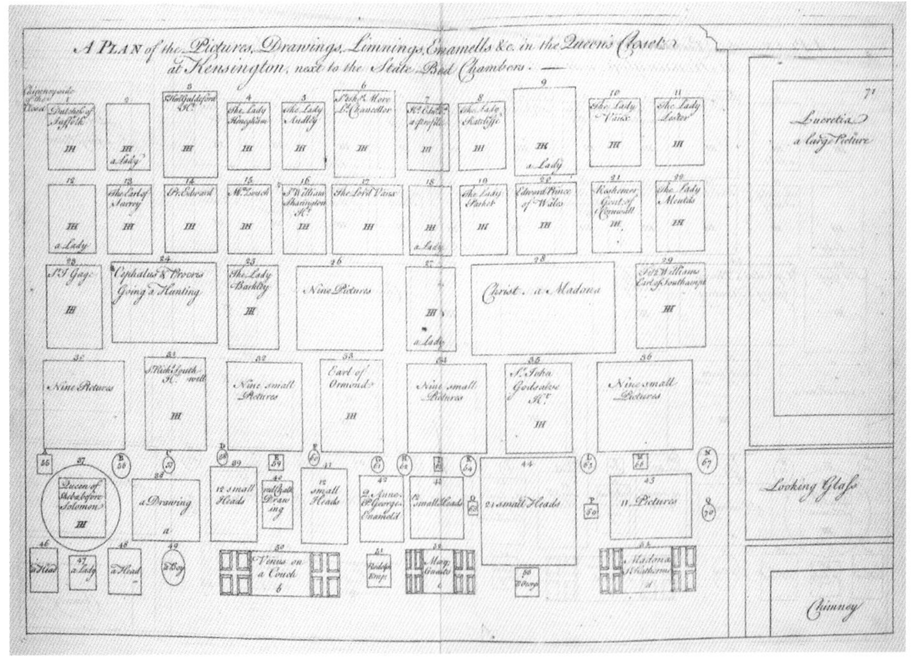

83. *(below) Plan of the picture hang in the 'Queen's Closet' at Kensington, as found in 1743.*

84. *(below, right) Anne Boleyn by Hans Holbein the Younger,* c. 1533–36. *According to Horace Walpole, this was one of a series of Holbein drawings found by Queen Caroline in 'a bureau in his Majesty's Great Closet'.*

85. The Fleet on the Serpentine River *after John Heaviside Clark, 1814. This line of miniature ships preparing for a sham sea fight was assembled to mark victories in the Napoleonic Wars.*

Tower menagerie (fig. 86). He also converted the rectangular pond to the east of the palace into the existing Round Pond.

The new Queen was determined to make the gardens surrounding the palace more accessible to the public. Bridgeman therefore swept away the formal gardens 'from the orangery down to the southern extent next the town' and replaced them with lawns, which gave visitors uninterrupted views across the park (figs. 89 and 90). Some wooded areas were cleared, and others were cut through with winding paths. By the end of 1728, a new Grand Walk had been created, running from north to south across the former park; it still survives today as the Broad Walk. As the Royal Gardener himself reflected in 1731, 'Their present majesties ... have made the whole into a garden by increasing the walking parts thereof.' Further east in the park, the Serpentine River was formed as a boating lake by flooding several smaller ponds (fig. 85). Ornamental buildings were added, including William Kent's revolving summer house on top of an earth mound and his Queen's Temple, an elegant little building on the western bank of the Serpentine with seats from which to admire the view (figs. 87 and 88).

86. Sketch of Charles Bridgeman, Royal Gardener between 1728 and 1738. Bridgeman was responsible for designing and managing the vast expansion of Kensington Gardens into Hyde Park.

Initial reactions to the new gardens were muted. Baron Pöllnitz, visiting in the early 1730s, reported, 'Kensington Gardens would be very fine for a private person, but for a King, methinks I could wish them to be somewhat more magnificent.' However, as they became more established, so did their popularity increase. In 1733 the *Gentleman's Magazine* published a poem in praise of the gardens:

> At ev'ry step, new scenes of beauty rise,
> Here, well judg'd vistas meet th'admiring eyes:
> A river there waves thro' the happy land,
> And ebbs and flows, at Caroline's command.

As the royal couple had intended, Kensington Gardens became invaluable as a place of entertainment and recreation. Public admission was controlled by gatekeepers, who excluded people

87. (right, top) The 'Mount', created by Charles Bridgeman in 1731–32 near the south-eastern corner of Kensington Gardens, looking southwards over Hyde Park. William Kent's stone-built 'seat' can be seen on top. The drawing, dated 1736, is by Bernard Lens the Younger.

88. (right) The Queen's Temple, the pavilion in Kensington Gardens designed by William Kent. View by John Buckler, 1828.

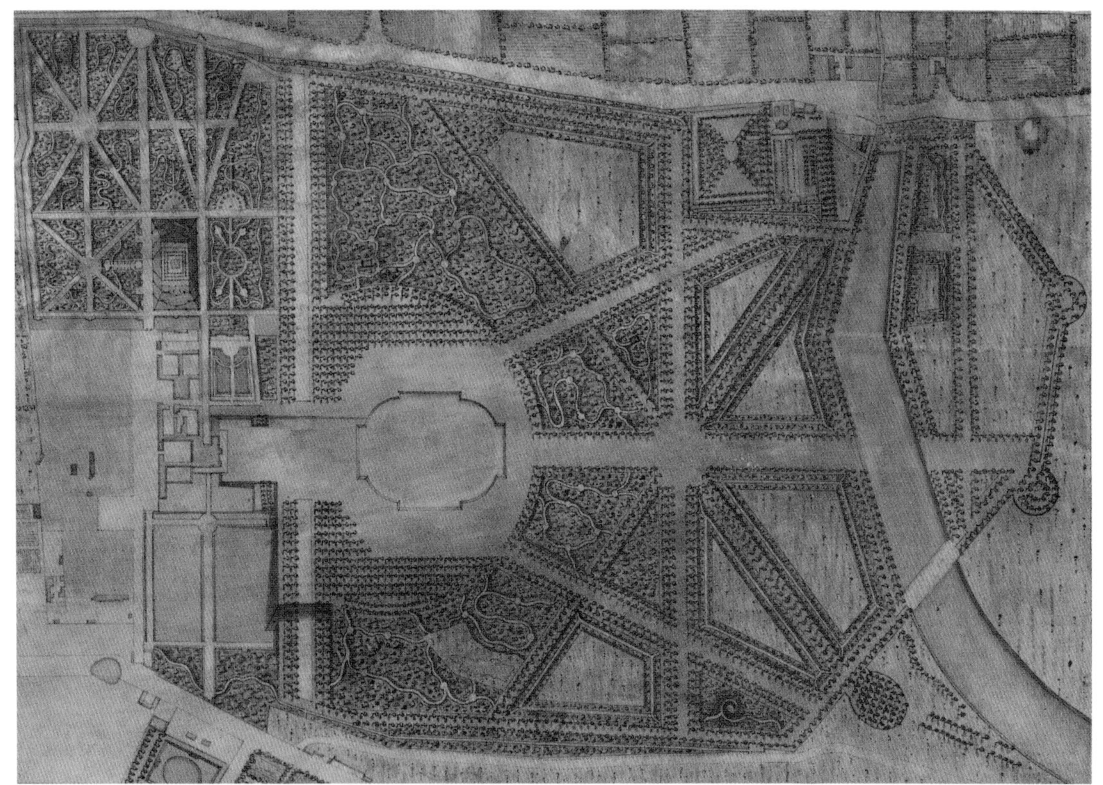

89. (left) Plan made for Charles Bridgeman in about 1733, showing Kensington Gardens on completion of the work begun in 1725. The main achievement of these years was the eastwards expansion of the gardens into Hyde Park. Most of the layout has since been lost, with the exception of the Serpentine (right), the Round Pond and the planting of the 'Great Bow' around it.

90. (below) View of the palace from the south-east, c. 1750. The vast lawn to the left, overlooked by the King's Gallery range, was laid out at Queen Caroline's request, replacing the elaborate gardens commissioned by William and Mary.

of ungenteel appearance. They were not always effective. Contemporary newspapers were filled with accounts of pickpockets and highwaymen attacking visitors on foot and ambushing carriages. George II himself was accosted by a political maniac in 1738, which prompted the introduction of military patrols to search the gardens 'as soon as the evening shuts in'.

Like their predecessor, George and Caroline soon established a routine of spending most summers at Kensington, usually moving there after the end of the parliamentary session in May or June. Even though he had tried to distance himself from his father when Prince of Wales, George soon began to emulate his other habits, including returning to Hanover for the summer, as he did in 1729 and on three subsequent occasions. Caroline acted as regent in his absence and conducted business in the King's State Apartments at Kensington.

An intelligent and cultured woman, Caroline was arguably better suited to the task of being sovereign than was her husband. Even when George was in London, ministers sought his wife's advice and direction. A popular verse declared,

> You may strut, dapper George, but 'twill all be in vain;
> We know 'tis Queen Caroline, not you, that reign.

91. John, Lord Hervey, after Jean-Baptiste van Loo, 1741. Hervey was a prominent figure during the reign of George II and was highly favoured by Queen Caroline. His memoirs, though not entirely reliable, provide a vivid depiction of life at the Georgian court.

The waspish courtier Lord Hervey, who served as Vice Chamberlain from 1730 to 1740, recalled, 'The whole world began to find out that her [Caroline's] will was the sole spring on which every movement in the Court turned. Her power was unrivalled and unabounded' (fig. 91). The Prime Minister, Robert Walpole, was particularly alive to the fact, and he and the Queen soon established a close working relationship. He privately reflected that, in courting her, he 'had the right sow by the ear'.

The other 'sow' was George II's long-standing (and long-suffering) mistress, Henrietta Howard (fig. 92). She had first attracted his attention in 1718, but theirs was an affair of convenience rather than passion. George was devoted to his wife, and seemed to 'look upon a mistress rather as a necessary appurtenance to his grandeur as a prince than an addition to his pleasures as a man', as Lord Hervey shrewdly observed. Renowned as a woman of wit and 'reason', Mrs Howard was the intellectual superior of her royal suitor and took far greater pleasure in the company of Alexander Pope,

John Gay and the other literary stars of the day. The fact that the King visited her apartments with the same clockwork regularity as his father had done with his mistress led courtiers to believe that she enjoyed a substantial degree of political influence, when in fact she had little.

By 1734 Henrietta had had enough. She created a scandal by being seen to converse with the King's political enemy, Viscount Bolingbroke, and resigned her position shortly afterwards. Ironically, Queen Caroline was more sorry to see her go than her husband was – perhaps because Henrietta had relieved her of George's company for several hours a day. When he found out that she had tried to persuade Henrietta to stay, the King exclaimed, 'What the devil did you mean by trying to make an old, dull, deaf, peevish beast stay and plague me when I had so good an opportunity of getting rid of her.' Caroline, meanwhile, was careful to show no disappointment at her failure to keep Henrietta at court, and declared, 'Her going from Court was the silliest thing she could do.'

By the time of Henrietta Howard's departure, court life at Kensington had fallen into the same predictable and rather dull routine

92. Henrietta Howard by Charles Jervas, c. 1724. George II's mistress for sixteen years, Henrietta was hailed as a 'woman of reason' and was friends with some of the greatest poets and artists of the age.

93. Inconveniences of a Crowded Drawing Room *by George Cruikshank, 1818. Among other things, Cruikshank ridicules the impracticality of court dress.*

established by George I. 'Dunce the second reigns like Dunce the first', sneered Pope in one of his most popular poems. The main public event was still the 'Drawing Room', which was held two or three times a week (fig. 93). A notorious incident took place during one such occasion in 1742. The Countess of Deloraine, who briefly replaced Mrs Howard as the King's mistress, suffered a prank when her chair was pulled away as she was sitting down. George found this so funny that the Countess did the same to him. 'Alas,' remarked Horace Walpole, 'the monarch, like Louis XIV, is mortal in the part that touched the ground, and was so hurt and so angry, that the Countess is disgraced.'

Another celebrated incident at Kensington involved the picture hang in the King's Drawing Room. George II was obsessed with detail and routine, and would notice if ever anything was out of place. During one of his visits to Hanover, Caroline rearranged the pictures to suit her tastes. When her husband returned, he spotted the change straight away and furiously demanded that the original selection be restored. Lord Hervey could not resist asking whether he would 'have the gigantic fat Venus [Vasari's *Venus and Cupid,* which still hangs in the room] restored too?' (fig. 94). When the King emphatically agreed, the courtier privately recorded that he 'thought, though he did not dare say, that, if His Majesty had liked his fat Venus [i.e. Caroline] as well as he used to do, there would have been none of these disputations'.

The King was still in a foul humour when he next appeared, as Lord Hervey recalled: '[He] stayed about five minutes in the gallery; snubbed the Queen, who was drinking chocolate, for being always stuffing, the Princess Emily [Amelia] for not hearing him, the Princess Caroline for being grown fat, the Duke [of Cumberland] for standing awkwardly, Lord Hervey for not knowing what relation the Prince of Sultzbach was to the Elector Palatine, and then carried the Queen to walk, and be resnubbed, in the garden.'

Harmony was soon restored, however, and the King and Queen resumed the customary round of social engagements at the palace. One of the more unusual took place in the summer of 1734, when a delegation of chiefs from the Creek tribe of North Americans arrived at Kensington. They had been brought over by James Oglethorpe, who had founded Savannah and the colony of Georgia in the King's name in the previous year. Oglethorpe persuaded them to wear more than the 'covering around their waist, the rest of the body being naked'. But they still presented an extraordinary sight to the King and his guests when they were received in the Presence Chamber with 'their faces ... variously painted after their country's manner, some half black, others triangular, and others with bearded arrows instead of whiskers'.

In November 1737 Queen Caroline was taken ill at St James's Palace with violent stomach pains. These were caused by an umbilical hernia

94. Venus and Cupid *by Giorgio Vasari,* c. 1543. *The painting was the subject of a famous row at Kensington between George II and Queen Caroline.*

that she had suffered after the birth of her last child in 1724. For two long weeks her distraught husband kept a constant vigil by her bedside. As she entered the final stages of her demise, Caroline urged George to marry again after she was dead. This threw him into a renewed fit of weeping, and in between sobs he spluttered, 'Non, j'aurai des maîtresses' [No, I will have mistresses], to which his wife sardonically replied, 'Ah! Mon Dieu! Cela n'empêche pas' [My God! That won't prevent your marrying].

Caroline's grief-stricken husband spent more time at Kensington after her demise. But life there had lost much of its glitter, and the King became increasingly reclusive. Horace Walpole reported that he 'has locked up half the palace since the Queen's death', and later reflected, 'At Kensington they have scarce company enough to pay for lighting the candles.'

One of the rare court celebrations took place in August 1743 to mark the victory of the allied forces at Dettingen. George had led his troops into battle – the last occasion that a reigning British monarch would ever do so. He was still in Bavaria when the crowds gathered in Kensington Gardens for a 'gala and rural illumination which darkened the stars'. It was a splendid occasion, as a newspaper reported: 'The palace was generally illuminated with wax lights etc. The trees at a distance in front of every angle were equally resplendent with lights. Music serenaded the company present, who were regaled with a cold collation on the stone pavement in front of the palace.'

Although he still missed his wife, George found increasing solace in the company of his children. His unmarried daughters Amelia and Caroline spent a great deal of time with him at the palace. This improved relations between them significantly, as the King himself reflected: 'I know I did not love my children when they were young, I hated to have them running into my room, but now I love them as well as most fathers.' His reconciliation with his eldest son and heir, Frederick, was short-lived, however. The Prince died in 1751 at the age of forty-four. The same 'fatal year', as the King termed it, saw the demise of his youngest daughter, Louisa. George found comfort in the arms of his last mistress, Amalie von Wallmoden, Countess of Yarmouth, who was observed to have 'sole and quite possession of her royal master' (fig. 95).

On the morning of 25 October 1760, the King rose, as usual, at 6 o'clock. He called for his hot chocolate, then walked over to the window overlooking the gardens at Kensington and declared that it was a fine day for a walk. A little after 7 o'clock, he retreated into

95. Engraving showing George II with his mistress, Amalie von Wallmoden, in 1738, a year after the death of his wife, Queen Caroline, whose portrait is shown in the centre. The King and his mistress were subjected to a certain amount of public ridicule.

the water closet, methodical as ever in his habits. His *valet de chambre*, waiting patiently outside while His Majesty completed his evacuations, was surprised by 'a noise louder than the royal wind', followed by a thud 'like the falling of a billet of wood from the fire'. He rushed in and found the King lying on the floor. There was a gash on his right temple caused by a heavy fall against the corner of a bureau, and his hand was stretched towards the bell that he had tried to ring for assistance. He whispered, 'Call Amelia', then spoke no more.

George II had been just shy of his seventy-seventh birthday when he suffered the aortic aneurysm that caused his demise. He was the last of four monarchs to die at the palace.

Kensington Palace, 1760–1837

George II's death drew to a close Kensington's brief period of prominence at the centre of court life. He was succeeded by his grandson, George III (1760–1820), son of the ill-fated Prince Frederick. The new King had avoided living at the palace as Prince of Wales, possibly because his parents had repudiated it after a terrible quarrel with George II and Caroline in 1735. Nor did he choose to reside there after his accession (fig. 97).

By the time of George III's accession in 1760, Kensington's architecture was considered to be out of fashion. Furthermore, its location did not suit the new King, who favoured such central London residences as the Queen's House (or Buckingham House, later known as Buckingham Palace) and country retreats such as Windsor and Kew (fig. 96). For the next thirty years, Kensington was, as one contemporary noted, 'entirely forsaken by the royal family'. It was maintained by only a small staff managed by the resident House and Wardrobe Keeper, who also acted as a tour guide to the large number of visitors.

By the end of the eighteenth century, the King faced growing criticism about the fact that he had abandoned Kensington as a royal palace, thus making the cost of its upkeep no longer justifiable. However, although he did not wish to live there himself, George had no desire to see it demolished. He therefore decided that the palace should be refurbished to provide accommodation for the junior members of the royal family. They included his fourth son, Prince Edward, later Duke of Kent, and his sixth, Prince Augustus Frederick, later Duke of Sussex, both of whom were bachelors (figs. 98 and 99). Prince Edward arrived first, in 1798, and was assigned the King's Private Apartments, while his brother later took over the entire courtiers' range. They were joined by

96. (right) The entrance front of Buckingham House as remodelled for George III by William Chambers in 1762–74. View by Thomas Sutherland after William Westall, from W.H. Pyne's History of the Royal Residences, *1819.*

97. (opposite, top) George III, Queen Charlotte and Their Six Eldest Children *by Johann Zoffany, 1770. Although the King and Queen did not live at Kensington themselves, three of their children – Edward, later Duke of Kent (fourth from left), the father of Queen Victoria; Augustus Frederick, later Duke of Sussex; and Sophia – made the palace their home in the early nineteenth century.*

98. (right) Prince Edward, Duke of Kent and Strathearn, by Johann Georg Paul Fischer, c. *1818. The Prince was allocated the King's Private Apartments at Kensington in 1798 and embarked on an extensive programme of building and decoration, kept up until his death in 1820.*

99. (far right) Prince Augustus Frederick, later Duke of Sussex, by Edward Miles, 1792–93. The sixth son of George III, the Duke lived at Kensington from 1806 until his death in 1843.

100. (above) Caroline of Brunswick by Sir Thomas Lawrence, 1804. George IV's unwanted Queen and mother of the tragically short-lived Princess Charlotte, Caroline lived at Kensington from 1808 to 1814.

101. (right) George IV by Sir Thomas Lawrence, 1821. George spent little time at Kensington and, like his father, George III, never used it as a residence. The fact that his estranged wife, Caroline, lived there made him even less inclined to visit the palace.

Caroline of Brunswick, who had separated from her husband, the Prince of Wales, later George IV (figs. 100 and 101). Increasingly isolated from the royal family, she established Kensington as a rival court and scandalized her brothers-in-law with her wild parties and eccentric behaviour.

The arrival of these new residents gave Kensington Palace a new sense of style and purpose. It also established what would become a long-standing tradition for young royals to make the palace their home. They were not all content, however. The Duke of Kent complained endlessly to his father about the poor condition into which his apartments had fallen, and his persistence resulted in a complete conversion of the lower floors of the palace – and years of wrangling over the cost of their repair (fig. 102). The King had also forbidden his son's mistress, Madame de St Laurent, to live at Kensington, which made the Duke even less inclined to spend time there.

All of this changed in 1817 with the death of Princess Charlotte, the only child of George III's eldest son, George, the Prince Regent. Next in line to the throne was George's brother Frederick, the Duke of York, who was married to a Prussian princess. But if the Duke remained childless, the throne would pass to the other brothers in order of seniority. This put pressure on the Duke of Kent to relinquish his bachelor lifestyle and marry for the sake of the succession.

The Duke's chosen bride was Victoria of Saxe-Coburg-Saalfeld, sister of Prince Leopold (Leopold I of Belgium from 1831), the widower of the late Princess Charlotte. They married in 1818, and after a brief stay at Kensington they went to live at the Duchess's ancestral seat at Amorbach. When she fell pregnant later that year, her husband decided that the child must be born in England, more precisely 'the old palace of our ancestors' – Kensington. He understood its symbolic importance to the Hanoverian dynasty, and went to desperate efforts to convey his wife, her daughter by her first marriage, Feodora, lapdogs and songbirds there in the late spring of 1819. They arrived in the nick of time, and their daughter was born on 24 May (fig. 103).

The Princess was christened at Kensington Palace, using the magnificent silver-gilt font made for Charles II in 1660 and now

102. The staircase built for the Duke of Kent in about 1807, linking Clock Court to the main rooms of his apartment.

103. Imagined view of the room in which Queen Victoria was born, by Percy Macquoid, 1899.

104. (opposite, top left) The Duchess of Kent and her daughter, Princess Victoria, by Sir William Beechey, 1821. The two-year-old Princess holds a miniature of her father, who had died in the previous year.

105. (opposite, top right) Princess Victoria, aged fifteen, by Carl Christian Vogel von Vogelstein, 1834. This drawing was made at Kensington Palace on 7 June, and Victoria later recorded in her journal: 'At ½ past 2 I sat to M. Vogel till a ¼ past 4.'

106. (opposite, bottom) View of Kensington Palace from the south-east by John Buckler, c. 1826. By this time, the palace was no longer used by the monarch but had a number of royal residents, including the young Princess Victoria and her mother.

displayed in the Jewel House at the Tower of London. Her uncle, the Prince Regent, who was suspicious of his brother and loathed the Duchess, insisted on a simple, private occasion. Mindful of his own daughter's recent death, he refused to allow either Charlotte or Augusta to be included among the names, but approved the Duke's choice of Alexandrina (after the child's godfather, Alexander I, Tsar of Russia) as the first and Victoria as the second.

A few months later, the Duke moved his family to Sidmouth for the winter. But on 23 January 1820 he died of pneumonia at the age of fifty-two, only six days before his father, George III. His widow and daughter returned to Kensington, penniless thanks to the considerable debts that the spendthrift Duke had accumulated (fig. 106). They would remain there until 1837, supported by an annual income from the Duchess's brother Prince Leopold (fig. 105). The new King, George IV (1820–30), continued to treat her with barely concealed contempt.

The infant Victoria was 'a pretty little princess, plump as a partridge' and, according to her late father, 'a pocket Hercules' (figs. 104 and 107). As she herself recalled, her earliest memories were of being at 'Kensington

Kensington Palace
June 7th 1834
Victoria
Kensington Palace May 24th 1819

107. (right) Princess Victoria playing with a dog during a stay in Ramsgate, by Lady Elizabeth Keith Heathcote, 1822–23. As Victoria later reflected, she was then 'very much indulged by everyone', and by all accounts already showed the determination and flashes of the 'Hanoverian' bad temper that she occasionally displayed as an adult.

108. (far right) Louise Lehzen, Princess Victoria's governess, drawn by the Princess in 1833. Sitting to the right is Victoria's beloved spaniel, Dash.

Palace where I can remember crawling on a yellow carpet that was set out for this purpose'. Recollecting his visit to Kensington in 1820, the politician William Wilberforce described the Princess as a 'fine animated child' who was busily occupied 'on the floor ... with its playthings, of which I soon became one'.

Although Victoria's childhood has often been depicted as an unhappy one, in part due to her own later recollections of the 'painful and difficult scenes' that took place there, she also cherished fond memories of the years that she spent in the 'poor old palace'. Until the age of five, she was in the charge of her nurse, Mrs Brock, by whom she was 'very much indulged'. Her care was then assigned to Louise Lehzen (later Baroness), governess of Victoria's half-sister, Princess Feodora. Lehzen would be a major influence on Victoria's development and would remain her closest confidante until the Princess's marriage in 1840 (fig. 108).

Princess Victoria's life at Kensington was governed by a regular, if unceremonial, routine. 'We lived in a very simple plain manner', she later recalled. 'Breakfast was at half past eight, luncheon at half past one, dinner at seven – to which I came generally (when it was no regular large dinner party) – eating my bread and milk out of a small silver basin.' Victoria's lessons were conducted from 9.30 in the morning until 6.00 in the evening (with a two-hour break in the middle of the day), and were superintended by professional tutors. Lehzen herself taught the Princess

109. Queen Victoria When a Girl *by Alexandre-Jean Dubois Drahonet, 1832. She is depicted outside Kensington Palace, her childhood home.*

110. (above) Princess Victoria's doll's house, which remained at Kensington after her departure on becoming Queen in 1837. Since 1899 the doll's house and other toys have been on display to the public in or near the rooms in which she lived as a child.

111. (top) Selection from among the 132 dolls dressed by Princess Victoria and her governess, Louise Lehzen, during the early 1830s. The designs of the dresses were based on those dresses worn by fashionable visitors or illustrated in women's journals, and some dolls were named after society figures.

history, however, and it was she who told her that she would one day be queen, prompting Victoria's famous declaration, 'I will be good.'

As a child, though, the Princess was often far from well behaved. Prone to explosive bursts of temper, she would stamp her feet when she did not get her way, and on one occasion she hurled a pair of scissors at her governess. Lehzen responded with kindness as well as discipline. She kept a 'Behaviour Book', in which her charge was variously described as 'very thoughtless', 'very naughty' and 'very impertinent'. Victoria later recalled that Lehzen 'devoted her life to me, from my fifth to my eighteenth year, with the most wonderful self-abnegation, never even taking one day's leave! ... I adored her, though I also feared her.'

The Princess enjoyed leisure time, too, and spent a great deal of it with her half-sister, Feodora, to whom she was very close, despite the twelve-year age gap. A visitor to Kensington Gardens saw the infant Princess as she 'skipped along between her mother and sister, the Princess Feodora, holding a hand of each'. Lehzen also played with Victoria, and often helped her to dress her collection of 132 dolls, for which they made tiny costumes (figs. 110 and 111). The Duchess, too, was more indulgent than has often been supposed. For example, at Christmas in 1832 her daughter noted in her diary, 'Mamma gave me a lovely pink bag which she had worked on herself with a little sachet likewise done by her ... and a pink satin dress and a cloak trimmed with fur.' Victoria also made the most of Kensington Gardens and Hyde Park, and was often seen in a carriage or, later, riding with surprising freedom (fig. 112).

The Princess often stayed with her adored Uncle Leopold at his house at Claremont in Surrey, which she described as 'the brightest epoch of my otherwise rather melancholy childhood'.

By contrast, another of her uncles, the Duke of Sussex, who still lived at Kensington, would often punish her. As a result, 'I always screamed when I saw him', Victoria recalled.

By far the most foreboding figure in the young Victoria's life, however, was her father's former friend and equerry Sir John Conroy (fig. 113). He had attended the Princess's birth and claimed that he had promised the dying Duke that his wife and daughter would be well cared for. The Duchess had quickly become dependent on him, and as her Chamberlain he soon controlled every aspect of her household, from expenditure on salaries to staff livery and routines.

Conroy also worked hard to ensure that his influence would continue once Victoria was queen. Inspired by this ambition, he and the Duchess engineered what became known as the 'Kensington System', a set of strict regulations to control the Princess. This ensured that she was kept away from court, resulting in worsening relations with George IV and then William IV, and she was also denied access to her mother's family, the Coburgs. The Princess was never allowed to be alone or to receive visitors without a third party being present. Nor could she walk down the stairs without holding an adult's hand. It was a suffocating system for the young Victoria, and her sense of isolation increased after the marriage of her beloved Feodora in 1828. The latter would later reflect, 'I escaped some years of imprisonment, which you, my poor dear Sister had to endure after I was married.'

The Princess took a step closer to the throne in June 1830, when George IV died and Victoria became heir presumptive (fig. 109). This prompted her mother to petition for accommodation that better suited Victoria's 'altered situation'. She complained to the Prime Minister, Charles Grey, that 'the Princess and myself are very inconveniently

112. (top) The ten-year-old Princess Victoria riding in a pony carriage in Kensington Gardens, with the East Front of the palace in the background, by John Doyle, 1829. The Princess was allowed remarkable freedom to ride and drive about the gardens, although always in the company of one or more grooms.

113. (above) Sir John Conroy by Henry William Pickersgill, 1837. As the confidant of Victoria's mother, the Duchess of Kent, Conroy was able to manoeuvre himself into a position of influence over the young Princess Victoria.

114. (below) The King's Gallery in 1816. By this time, the State Apartments had not been put to any formal use since 1760, but they still retained a large part of the furniture and pictures that had been there at that date. View by Thomas Sutherland after Charles Wild, from W.H. Pyne's History of the Royal Residences, *1819.*

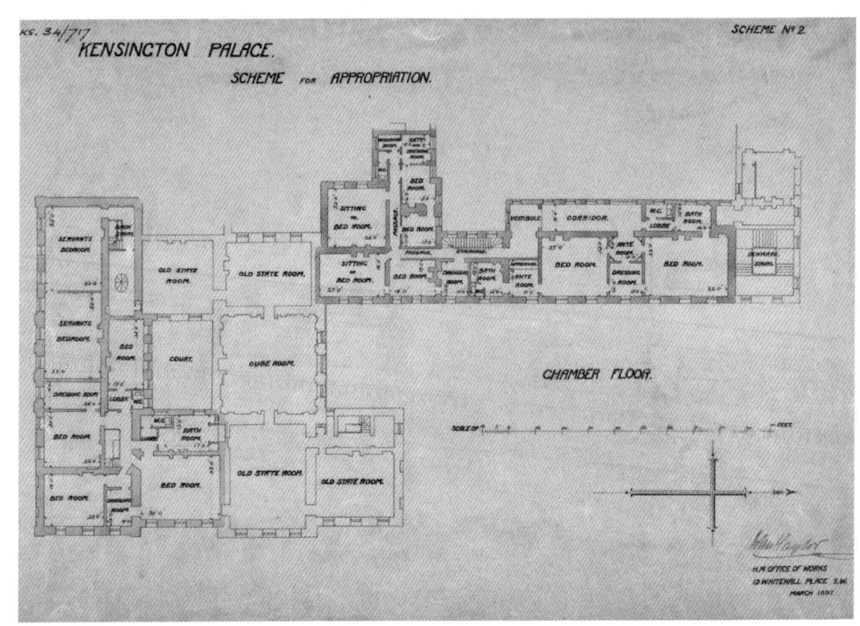

115. (right) Plan of the palace at State Apartment level, showing the partitions inserted into the former King's Gallery for the Duchess of Kent and her daughter in 1835. The plan was prepared in 1897 to show part of the accommodation then being proposed for Princess Beatrice, Queen Victoria's youngest daughter.

116. (left) Dash, Princess Victoria's favourite pet, in a painting probably given to her by Sir John Conroy on her fourteenth birthday. Victoria made suits of clothes for her spaniel, including a 'scarlet coat and blue trousers'. Painting by George Morley, 1833–35.

117. (below) Princess Victoria's bedroom. It was here that the eighteen-year-old Princess was awoken in the early hours of 20 June 1837 with the news that her uncle William IV had died and she was now Queen.

and inadequately lodged here', and suggested they take over the State Apartments, which were 'unoccupied or used for old pictures' (fig. 114).

But relations between the Duchess and the new King, William IV (1830–37), were already strained, thanks in part to her preventing Victoria from attending his coronation because her place in the procession was behind his brothers instead of directly after the King. William was said to be 'very jealous' when he heard of his sister-in-law's plans for Kensington, but she forged ahead regardless. Although he conceded that she could move into the State Apartments on condition that they remained at his disposal and in their present form, she immediately set about a radical transformation of the rooms. Much of the work had been completed by 1836, when Princess Victoria enthused, 'Our bedroom is very large and lofty, and is very nicely furnished, then comes a little room for the maid, and a dressing-room for Mamma; then comes the old gallery which is partitioned into three large, lofty, fine and cheerful rooms' (figs. 115 and 117).

The Princess and her mother made full use of the newly refurbished apartments, hosting a round of glittering balls and receptions. In May 1836 they received a visit from Victoria's cousin Prince Albert. This had been engineered

118. Queen Victoria receiving the news of her accession at Kensington Palace, early in the morning of 20 June 1837, as imagined by Henry Tanworth Wells in 1880. Kneeling to the right is the Archbishop of Canterbury, William Howley, and to the left the Lord Chamberlain, Lord Conyngham. When she was shown the painting, Victoria remarked, 'Lord Conyngham who is kneeling should not have a grey coat but a black one. His hair was very dark not reddish. The Archbishop should not have a Cloak on but the usual dress of a Bishop.'

by their uncle King Leopold and the Duchess, who considered Albert an ideal husband for the Princess. Victoria was delighted with the young Prince, and on the day of their first meeting she recorded in her journal that he was 'extremely handsome; his hair is about the same colour as mine; his eyes are large and blue, and he has a beautiful nose and a very sweet mouth' (fig. 119). She concluded that he was 'full of goodness and sweetness and very clever and intelligent'. Albert charmed Victoria by playing 'so funnily' with her beloved King Charles spaniel, Dash, but he was exhausted by the dizzying round of social engagements that the Duchess had planned for his visit (fig. 116). On 24 May, at a celebration held for Victoria's birthday, Albert stayed 'a short while in the ball-room and having only danced twice, turned as pale as ashes' and went home early.

In August of that year, King William IV paid a visit to Kensington so that he might inspect the alterations. Aghast that the Duchess had 'appropriated' no fewer than seventeen apartments, he loudly and publicly castigated her, declaring – in the words of the diarist Charles Greville – that 'a most unwarrantable liberty had been taken with one of his palaces; that he had just come from Kensington, where he found apartments had been taken possession of not only without his consent, but contrary to his commands'.

The next day, his birthday (21 August), the King made a speech in which he expressed the hope that he would live until Victoria turned eighteen so that she would succeed as queen and not be placed under a regency led by her mother and her 'evil advisers'. His wish would be granted. He died very early in the morning of 20 June 1837, one month after the Princess's birthday.

As soon as the King had breathed his last at Windsor, the Lord Chamberlain and the Archbishop of Canterbury set out for Kensington (fig. 118). Victoria described their arrival:

> I was awoke at 6 o'clock by Mamma who told me that the archbishop of Canterbury and Lord Conyngham were here and wished to see me. I got out of bed and went into my sitting room (only in my dressing gown) and alone, and saw them. Lord Conyngham then acquainted me that my poor Uncle, the King, was no more ... and consequently that I am Queen.

The Duchess of Kent and her Chamberlain were quick to try to assert their influence over the new Queen. 'Do not be too sanguine in your own talents and understanding', urged Victoria's mother. Conroy, meanwhile, condescendingly observed that she was 'younger in intellect than in years'. But Victoria was determined to throw off their suffocating restrictions now that she was the monarch. She carried out her first public duties alone. At 9 o'clock the same morning, she received the Prime Minister, Lord Melbourne, and confirmed that she wished to keep him in office. She then presided over a meeting of the Privy Counsellors in what is now called the Red Saloon. 'I went in of course quite alone', she reflected with satisfaction.

'Her extreme youth and inexperience, and the ignorance of the world concerning her, naturally excited intense curiosity', observed Charles Greville. But the young Queen soon proved her mettle. On entering the Red Saloon, 'She bowed to the Lords, took her seat, and then read her speech in a clear, distinct and audible voice, and without any appearance of fear or embarrassment ... She went through the whole ceremony ... with perfect calmness and self-possession, but at the same time

119. Etching of Prince Albert by Queen Victoria, 1840. Princess Victoria first met her future husband at Kensington Palace in 1836.

120. (below) Queen Victoria's first Privy Council meeting, as depicted by Sir David Wilkie in 1838. It was held at 11 a.m. in the Red Saloon at Kensington Palace on the day of her accession. To make her stand out, the artist shows the Queen wearing a white dress, but – being in mourning for the King – she actually wore a black one.

121. *(right)* Buckingham Palace with Marble Arch *by John Buckler, 1835. Queen Victoria moved into Buckingham Palace in July 1837 and within a few years had ordered extensive building work to provide more space for accommodation and entertaining. As part of this redevelopment, the triumphal arch, now known as Marble Arch, was moved to the north-eastern corner of Hyde Park.*

with a graceful modesty and propriety particularly interesting and ingratiating.' Even the formidable military leader the Duke of Wellington was impressed. 'She was as gracious in her manner as if she had been performing the part for years', he recorded (figs. 120 and 122).

Although there had been some speculation that Victoria would remain at Kensington once she became Queen, she soon made it clear that she had no intention of doing so. Instead, she chose Buckingham Palace, where John Nash had begun an ambitious programme of improvements during George IV's reign (fig. 121). It was a decisive break with the past – and, more specifically, with her mother and the dreadful Conroy.

Victoria spent her last night at Kensington on 12 July 1837. The palace had become more like a prison in recent years, but she still cherished some fondness for it, as she confided to her Uncle Leopold:

> It is not without feelings of regret that I shall bid adieu for ever (that is to say for ever as a dwelling), to this my birth-place, where I have been born and bred, and to which I am really attached! I have seen my dear sister married here, I have seen many of my dear relations here, I have had pleasant balls and delicious concerts here, my present rooms upstairs are really very pleasant, comfortable and pretty ... I have gone through painful and disagreeable scenes here, 'tis true, but I am still fond of this poor old Palace.

122. The dress that Queen Victoria wore for her first Privy Council meeting is now preserved in the Royal Ceremonial Dress Collection at Kensington Palace. The black silk of the mourning dress has faded to brown.

Victorian Kensington, 1837–99

Even before Queen Victoria had left her childhood home, much of it had fallen into a state of disrepair. One of the Queen's aunts, Princess Sophia, was obliged to move out for a few years because of its 'ruinous condition' (fig. 123). Her death in 1848, and that of her brother the Duke of Sussex five years earlier, brought to a close the palace's occupation by George III's children (fig. 124). The only remaining link with that generation was the Duke of Sussex's widow, Cecilia, who continued to live there until her death in 1873.

But thanks in no small part to Victoria's lingering affection for the palace, Kensington was far from abandoned (figs. 125 and 126). Indeed, it continued to be an important home for the younger generation of the royal family – notably Victoria's children the Princesses Louise and Beatrice, her cousin Princess Mary Adelaide and the latter's husband, the Duke of Teck.

The Tecks were the first to arrive, in July 1867. The Duchess, Mary Adelaide, was a first cousin of the Queen. Amiable, popular and

123. (right, top) Princess Sophia by Anthony Stewart, c. 1822–23. Born in 1777, Sophia was the twelfth child of George III and Queen Charlotte. Except for a five-year period when the palace was under repair, she occupied an apartment at Kensington from 1820 until her death in 1848.

124. (right) Visitors to the lying-in-state of the Duke of Sussex in 1843. Up to 20,000 people arrived at the palace to pay their respects and left via a temporary staircase, descending from a window in the King's Gallery range.

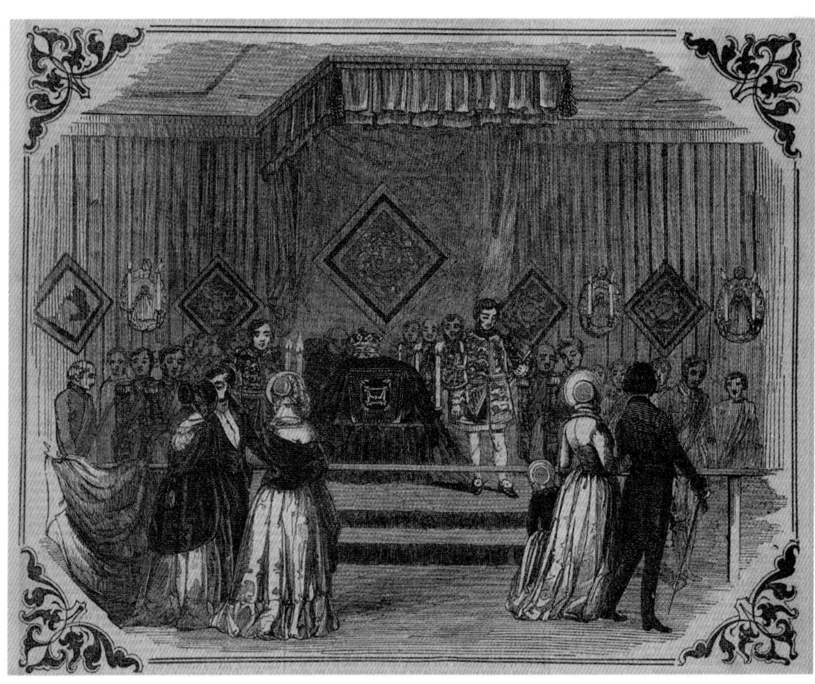

125. View of the Mews, Kensington Palace, c. 1868–71.

126. Colonel Chaine and his wife, Maria (née Phipps), Kensington's State Housekeeper, photographed in 1897 outside their apartment in Clock Court. Mrs Chaine had few real duties, but lived at Kensington with a substantial household from 1867 until 1915.

127. Princess Louise, Duchess of Argyll, by Philip Alexius de László, 1915. The Princess lived at Kensington from 1875 until 1939.

generously proportioned, she was known affectionately as 'Fat Mary'. Mary had married Prince Francis (Franz) of Teck, only son of Duke Alexander of Württemberg, in 1866, and her husband was granted the status of Duke of Teck five years later. As the couple had few resources of their own, Victoria allowed them to occupy her former apartments at Kensington. These had been used for storage since the Queen's departure thirty years earlier, so they were in need of repair and redecoration (fig. 128).

Shortly after the Tecks' arrival, their first daughter was born in the former King's Bedchamber. Victoria described her visit to the new baby: 'Franz received me at the door, and we went up to the top of the house, where I lived the last two years; and here, in the former bedroom, in which Mamma and I slept, I found dear Mary, Aunt Cambridge and the baby – a very fine child' (fig. 129).

The Tecks grew very fond of Kensington, but their dire finances forced them to leave for Florence in 1882. By then, however, the palace was notable for another resident: Princess Louise, the most talented and least conventional of the Queen's five daughters (fig. 127). Born at Buckingham Palace in 1848, Louise was Queen Victoria's and Prince Albert's sixth child and fourth daughter. From an early age, she displayed a considerable talent for drawing and painting, which her parents, both accomplished artists, actively encouraged.

Prince Albert's sudden death from typhoid in December 1861 had a devastating effect on the royal family. Victoria was grief-stricken by the loss of the husband she adored, and she went into a period of intense and prolonged mourning. Albert had been a very active consort, supporting his wife with a whole host of her royal duties. This burden fell to Princess Louise on the marriage in 1866 of her elder sister Helena, which left the eighteen-year-old Louise as the eldest unmarried daughter in the house. The Princess acted as her mother's unofficial secretary and companion, and among her less onerous duties were the sketching trips that she and Queen Victoria made to the Highlands of Scotland and to Switzerland.

Much as she loved her daughter, Victoria was increasingly alarmed by Louise's growing feminism and liberalism, so in 1868 she began searching for a suitable husband for her. In October 1870 Louise became engaged to the twenty-five-year-old John Campbell, Marquess of Lorne, while he was visiting Balmoral at the invitation of

128. The Duchess of Teck's Morning Room, c. 1868–71. The Duke and Duchess lived at Kensington from 1867 until 1882, and their first daughter, later Queen Mary, was born there soon after they arrived.

129. The Duke and Duchess of Teck with Princess Mary (on the Duke's knee) in their garden at Kensington, facing the palace's East Front, in 1868.

130. Princess Louise's statue of Queen Victoria in her coronation robes, commissioned to mark her mother's Golden Jubilee in 1887, was unveiled in the Queen's presence in 1893. Louise's friend Alfred Gilbert – best known for the Eros statue in Piccadilly – may have had a hand in the design.

131. (below) Queen Victoria at the unveiling of her daughter Louise's statue of her in Kensington Gardens, 1893.

132. (right) Drawing showing the two studios built for Princess Louise in the small walled garden to the south of her apartment. The lower building (shown at the centre) was erected in 1878 and survived for the remainder of her life. The taller building was destroyed when a tree fell down in 1922.

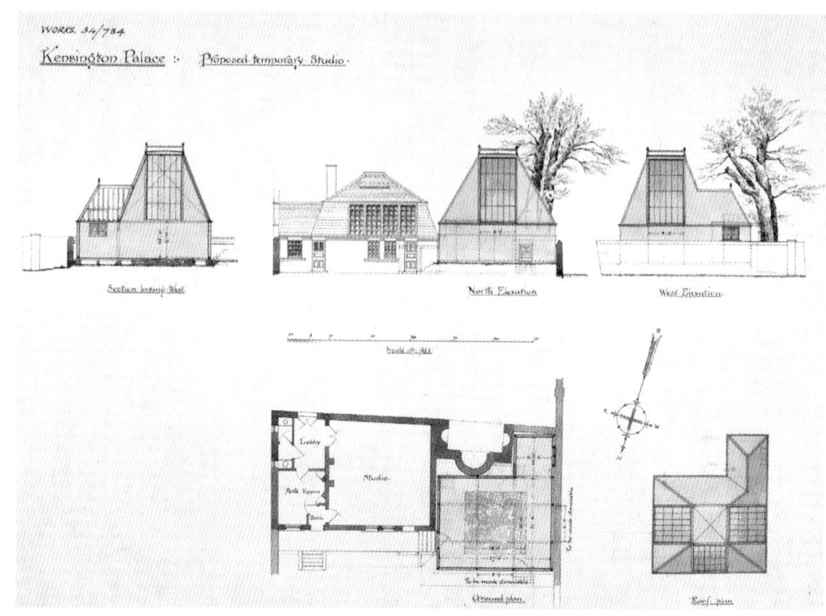

the Queen. Louise was hardly smitten, but she at least found Campbell more acceptable than the various foreign princes whom her mother had suggested. They were married in the following March. Although she had arranged the match, Victoria found it hard to let her daughter go, confiding in her journal that she 'felt painfully the thought of losing her'.

After the death of the Duke of Sussex's widow two years later, Louise and Lorne were given the use of Apartment 1 at Kensington, and moved there in February 1875. Queen Victoria was delighted that her daughter was now living in her old home, and wrote to Louise after a visit: 'I can't tell you the feeling it gave me to see my old Bedroom and the old doors – and the very view I knew so well – and then downstairs to the old rooms where so many lived – including dear Papa!' The apartment was vast but somewhat dilapidated, and Louise and her husband soon embarked on a programme of repair and redecoration.

By now, Louise was an artist of some renown, and was particularly distinguished for her sculptures (fig. 132). In 1868 a bust of her brother Prince Arthur was displayed by the Royal Academy. Her most celebrated work, though, was the white marble statue of her enthroned mother, which was commissioned to mark the Queen's Golden Jubilee in 1887. Victoria visited her daughter's studio at Kensington Palace 'to see the colossal statue she is doing of me in my coronation robes for Kensington ... The statue is really wonderfully executed, for she has done it alone, and worked very hard on it ... It will soon be ready to be cast.' The statue was installed six years later in the gardens to the east of the palace (figs. 130 and 131). It still sits there today and, thanks to recent renovation work, is every bit as splendid as when it was first unveiled.

Louise had been assisted in this commission by the Hungarian artist Joseph Edgar Boehm, and there were rumours of an affair. Her marriage to John Campbell was not a happy one, and he was widely thought to

133. (above) The Stone Gallery, originally the main link between the entrance to Kensington Palace and the State Apartments, c. 1900. *At that time it was incorporated in Princess Louise's apartment and was later used by Princess Margaret and Lord Snowdon.*

134. (left) The drawing room of Princess Louise's apartment at Kensington, on the south side of Clock Court, photographed in 1940, shortly after her death. In 1961–62 part of this apartment, including the room shown here, was refurbished for Princess Margaret and Lord Snowdon, becoming Apartment 1A.

be gay; certainly, they had no children. Louise and Boehm were alone in his Fulham Road studio when he suddenly died in December 1890. The press speculated that they had been making love when Boehm collapsed, but the Princess later attested that he had suffered a heart attack while staggering under the weight of a large sculpture.

During the First World War, by which time her husband had died, Louise converted part of her apartment at Kensington into a hospital and stepped up her involvement in charitable causes. During the course of her long life, she had built up a vast range of correspondents, including many of the best-known artists of the day, among them Sir John Everett Millais and James McNeill Whistler. Even in old age she remained very knowledgeable about politics and current affairs (fig. 135).

When the Second World War broke out in 1939, Princess Louise was ninety-one years old and refused to leave Kensington Palace. A suite of concrete rooms at the eastern-most end of her apartment was therefore fitted up as an air-raid shelter. In the event, they were not required because the Princess died on 3 December 1939, just three months after war had been declared (fig. 134). Her great-niece, the Duchess of Argyll, described her as 'one of the nicest people I have ever known'.

If Louise had – understandably – refused to leave Kensington, then her younger sister, Beatrice (then aged eighty-two), proved more compliant. She was evacuated to Brantridge Park, a 'little house in Sussex', and lived there until her death in October 1944.

Beatrice had taken up residence at Kensington on her mother's death in 1901. Before then, she had been obliged to live with the Queen, who had made no secret of the fact that Beatrice was her favourite child. In 1885 her mother had eventually – and with great reluctance – agreed

135. Princess Louise welcoming her battalion, the 13th London Regiment, to Kensington Palace on their return from training camp, 11 August 1935. The photograph shows the battalion giving three cheers for the Princess.

that she could marry Prince Henry of Battenberg, but only on condition that Beatrice (and her new husband) continued to live with her. The marriage was a happy one and resulted in the birth of four children, but it was cut tragically short by the Prince's death in 1896, on an expedition to West Africa.

Queen Victoria had allocated Beatrice the apartment that she herself had formerly occupied. But by 1901 this was in 'a very dilapidated wretched state', as Beatrice herself noted in a letter to Reginald Brett, 2nd Viscount Esher. He was one of Queen Victoria's most devoted courtiers and, as Permanent Secretary to the Office of Works, took on the task of making the apartment fit for purpose. 'I am glad to think that my having a pied a terre in London is now settled ... I am very much indebted to you for helping the matter', Beatrice wrote to him. 'No doubt in some ways Kensington has its advantages, and since there is nothing else more central to be obtained I am much relieved that this has been able to be settled.'

Beatrice would live there for almost forty years (fig. 136). During her residence, she occupied herself with, among other things, transcribing her mother's voluminous papers, in the process destroying and distorting much of the material to avoid any scandal if ever they came to light.

136. One of the rooms formerly occupied by Princess Beatrice, photographed just after her departure in 1940. She was the last royal resident of this side of the palace.

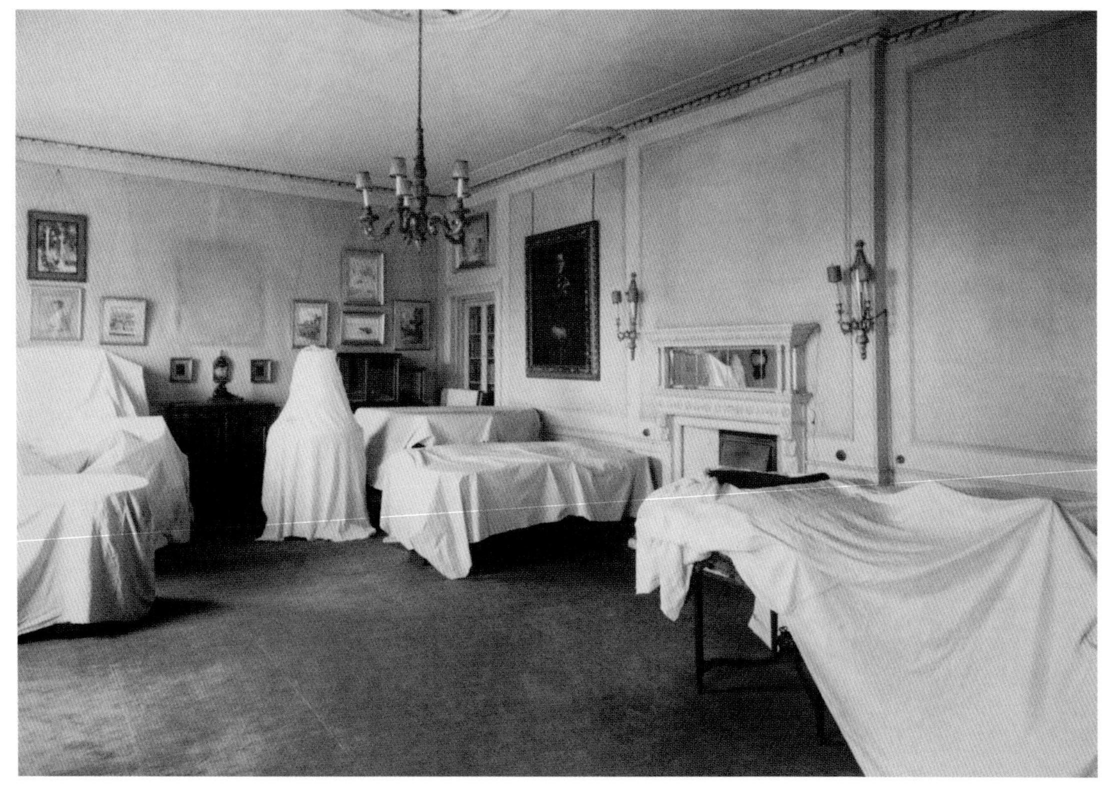

137. (below) The Crystal Palace Seen from the Serpentine *by William Wyld, 1852. The palace was built on the south side of Hyde Park to house the Great Exhibition of 1851, which was championed by Queen Victoria's beloved husband, Albert, and became one of the spectacular success stories of Victorian England. At the time, space was made available in Kensington Palace for the police and others involved in putting up the Crystal Palace and managing the exhibition.*

138. (opposite) The east side of the Queen's Gallery range, as depicted in The Graphic *on 1 July 1893, shored up to prevent its collapse. After decades of neglect, the State Apartments were by then in a very dilapidated and dangerous condition. This article reflected a growing public interest in London's monuments, and gave impetus to the decision to restore the palace.*

The State Apartments had been open to the public for two years by the time Princess Beatrice took up residence. Prince Albert had once expressed anxiety that his 'poor children would be turned into the streets' if the palace became too much of a visitor attraction, but his fears proved unfounded. By the dawn of the twentieth century, the State Apartments and private royal residences coexisted harmoniously, and continue to do so to this day.

The idea that Kensington Palace should be put to other uses, besides serving as a royal residence, in order to help fund its upkeep had been mooted since the mid-nineteenth century (fig. 137). There had even been calls to demolish it altogether and build a new national gallery in its place. When the plan was put to Victoria in 1852, she had sent a masterful reply to the Prime Minister, Lord John Russell, protesting that she did 'not see why it should be placed upon the site of the present Palace, if not for the purpose of taking from the Crown the last available set of apartments'. She added that she would 'not object to its being built on to Kensington Palace or anywhere in Kensington Gardens'.

Victoria had successfully fended off the idea for the time being, but during the years that followed Kensington remained a target for

other schemes. The unavoidable issue was that much of the palace – the State Apartments in particular – was in a poor state of repair and the Treasury was unwilling to spend money on its restoration (fig. 138). In 1898 *The Times* published an article praising the Queen's protection of her old home: 'More than once it has been seriously proposed to pull the whole building down, and to deal otherwise with the land, and Her Majesty's subjects ought to be grateful to her for having strenuously resisted such an act of Vandalism, and for having declared that, while she lived, the palace in which she was born should not be destroyed.'

By that time, a solution had finally been settled upon, thanks to the Queen's desire to find a suitable house for her daughters Beatrice and Helena. In 1897 a deal was struck whereby the government agreed to fund the restoration of the Princesses' apartments, as well as the 'State Rooms' and the Orangery, and in return Victoria would make Kew Palace, Queen Charlotte's Cottage (also at Kew) and the Ranger's Lodge at Greenwich available for sale or lease. The Queen formally approved the scheme, to the effect that 'Her Majesty desired that the State Rooms of Kensington Palace, which have been unoccupied since October 1760, should be put into proper repair and returned as nearly as possible to their former condition, with a view to their being opened to the Public during her Majesty's Pleasure.'

An extensive programme of restoration followed, under the general supervision of Sir John Taylor, the Surveyor of Royal Palaces, Public Buildings and Royal Parks for the Ministry of Works. Taylor had previously superintended major restoration work at the Tower of London, which involved needlessly destroying much of the important medieval fabric. He was therefore cautioned that at Kensington he should 'adhere

139. *(above) The West Front of Kensington Palace by F. Walter Lee, 1894.*

140. *(right) The King's Drawing Room as it appeared at the opening of the palace to the public in 1899. The intention was to evoke the mid-eighteenth-century appearance of the State Apartments and to present the building, in the words of Reginald Brett (later Lord Esher), 'as a Palace not a picture gallery'.*

141. (above, left) Queen Victoria arrives to inspect the restoration of Kensington Palace, 15 May 1899. From The Illustrated London News, *20 May 1899.*

142. (above) Front cover of the musical score for 'The Kensington Polka' by G.F. Anderson, late nineteenth century. By this time the palace had become part of popular culture.

strictly to the details of which we have record so that the decoration when complete may appear as far as possible exactly what it was in the reign of George II'.

Taylor heeded the warning. In his 1898 *Guidebook* to Kensington, the historian Ernest Law noted approvingly that 'never before ... has the restoration of any historic public building been carried out with quite the same amount of loving care'. He added that careful attention had been paid 'never to renew any decoration where it was possible to preserve it – least of all ever to attempt to "improve" old work into new'. This approach made the restoration of Kensington a landmark in the conservation of historic buildings and their presentation to the public.

The press were allowed a preview of the works in January 1898. *The Times* enthused that the result had been 'to endow London with another Hampton Court', but stressed that 'Kensington remained a Royal Palace to be occupied at any time by the Sovereign ... not a public building handed over for the perpetual enjoyment of the public.' The Queen herself came to inspect the restoration on 15 May 1899, and nine

143. (above) Illustration by Arthur Rackham for J.M. Barrie's Peter Pan in Kensington Gardens, *1906. Children are shown playing in the snow-covered avenue to the west side of the south gardens. Barrie's works have brought Kensington Gardens to life for generations of children, and since 1912 Peter Pan himself has been represented by a statue on the west side of the Serpentine.*

144. (right) Yachting at Kensington*: a man and a young boy launch model schooners on the Round Pond, with the palace in the background. Illustration from* The Boy's Own Paper, *late nineteenth century.*

145. Visitors to Kensington admire displays of Queen Victoria's doll's house and other toys, c. *1900.*

days later the palace was opened to the public (figs. 140 and 141). It was an instant success, with more than 340,000 visitors in the first year (figs. 142 and 145).

The use and popularity of Kensington Gardens also increased rapidly (fig. 143). From the mid-nineteenth century onwards, the gardens had served as a promenade for pram-pushing nannies, and by the 1870s the Round Pond was a celebrated meeting place for model-boat enthusiasts (figs. 144 and 146). Improved visitor facilities were provided, including the first refreshment room in 1855 and, in 1899, the first public lavatories.

146. Nannies pushing prams outside Kensington Gardens, 1933. From the mid-nineteenth century, the gardens became a popular place for nannies and nursery maids to bring their young charges for fresh air and exercise.

The Palace in the Twentieth Century

Kensington's history as a visitor attraction took a new turn in 1911, when it became the first home of the London Museum, now known as the Museum of London (fig. 147). This museum was the brainchild of the Liberal MP Lewis Harcourt, First Commissioner of Works from 1905 to 1910 and a friend of Lord Esher. He argued that London deserved something akin to the Musée Carnavalet in Paris, which told the story of the city from the earliest times to the early 1800s.

Thanks to Esher's support, by 1910 Harcourt was already buying exhibits and investigating possible locations, but he soon found that he could not afford a suitable building. When his friend received a letter from the Queen Mother, Alexandra, it sparked an idea. Alexandra had written to ask Esher's advice on a suitable home for a collection of relics of Queen Victoria and her recently deceased husband, King Edward VII (1901–10), that she wished to give to the nation as a memorial. Esher wasted no time in proposing that these treasures be amalgamated with Harcourt's artefacts and put on display in the State Apartments at Kensington Palace.

Alexandra was delighted with the idea and enlisted the support of her daughter-in-law, Queen Mary, in persuading her son, George V (1910–36), to agree. The idea chimed with Mary's desire to increase access to the Royal Collection and to make the palace a vehicle for public good. Her support for the London Museum at Kensington was exemplary of her subtle yet effective political role in shaping the monarchy and public attitudes to it. Her husband's reign saw unprecedented social

147. The secretary, F.A. Harman Oates (left), and typist, Maurice Read, photographed in the London Museum's first office at Kensington Palace, 1911.

148. Bronze statue of William III by the German sculptor Heinrich Baucke, presented to Edward VII in 1907 by the King's nephew Kaiser Wilhelm II and installed on the South Front of the palace.

149. The Sunken Garden, which was installed immediately to the east of the palace in 1908–1909. For the previous thirty or so years, the site had been occupied by cold frames and greenhouses, used for bringing on bedding plants for use elsewhere in the gardens.

and political change, but the fact that the monarchy emerged with its reputation enhanced was in no small measure due to the Queen's public spiritedness.

Thanks to numerous gifts, purchases and finds from City building sites, the new museum's collection expanded rapidly (fig. 150). Its main focus was on artefacts of everyday life and work, rather than on quality and craftsmanship. Queen Mary wholeheartedly supported this approach. 'It is a pity to get too fine things for the Museum', she told Lord Esher. 'The charm to me of the London Museum is seeing amusing little things connected with our city which one cannot see elsewhere. It is not to go in for beauty so much.'

During the course of 1911, the entire State Apartments were filled with cases crammed full of 'objects of historic and local interest to Londoners', as *The Times* put it, including relics of daily life from prehistoric to Tudor times, such as kitchen utensils, old coins, weapons and shoes, as well as 'fancy pottery' from Queen Mary's collection (fig. 151). After a royal preview in March 1912, the museum was opened to the public and a staggering 13,000 visitors were admitted on the first day alone (fig. 152). The museum's Keeper,

150. One of the most popular exhibits at the London Museum, the remains of a supposedly Roman boat, found during the construction of London's new County Hall and exhibited in a purpose-built annexe at Kensington from 1911 to 1913.

151. The King's Gallery, filled with the London Museum's exhibits, c. *1912.*

152. *The royal party that visited the London Museum on 21 March 1912, shown here inspecting exhibits in the Cupola Room. King George V (left) is listening to Lewis Harcourt; to the extreme right is the Keeper, Guy Laking, standing beside Queen Mary, Princess Mary and Prince George (later Duke of Kent).* The Times *reported that the King was in a 'merry mood' and thoroughly enjoyed the visit.*

Guy Laking, told Harcourt that it 'is nothing short of astonishing, indeed the queues waiting to get in, suggest the attractions of a musical comedy or football match, rather than visitors calmly viewing a museum'. Among the most popular exhibits were items of royal dress that had been loaned by Queen Alexandra.

Despite its success, the museum soon outgrew its Kensington home, and it was moved to Lancaster House in St James's after just a year. The State Apartments were then closed to the public, partly as a precautionary measure to protect the palace's collections from violent suffragette demonstrators, who had wreaked havoc at several London museums. During the First World War, they underwent another

153. Kensington Gardens in War-time *by Edith M. Bainbrigge, 1914, showing a military camp beside the Round Pond.*

incarnation as the home of various charitable organizations, such as the Sailors' and Soldiers' Christmas Fund and the Irish Women's Association (fig. 153).

After a decade of closure, the State Apartments were finally opened to the public again in 1923. The previous year, the First Commissioner of Works, David Lindsay, Earl of Crawford and Balcarres, had visited the palace and was 'agreeably surprised' by what he saw. 'It is true that the place has the unoccupied and somewhat derelict appearance of a noble suite of apartments which has long been abandoned,' he wrote, 'but even taking into account the quality of the pictures, the absence of furniture, and a certain grubbiness, I cannot help thinking that with a very little trouble ... these apartments could be opened to the public without appreciable cost to our Votes. Apart from the interest in seeing the apartments themselves, which offer a pleasing contrast of intimacy and stateliness, I was struck by the extraordinary variety of views from the different windows.'

Initially, the palace was open only on Saturday afternoons and visitors were charged sixpence. However, opening times were gradually extended, and by the mid-1930s the State Apartments could be visited every day of the week from March to September. Their popularity was due in no small part to the opening up of the 'Victorian rooms' by Queen Mary in the apartment in which she and Queen Victoria had lived as children. These included the bedroom in which Victoria had been born, the adjoining anteroom and the dressing

154. (left) The Duchess of Kent's Dressing Room, as redecorated and furnished in 1936 on Queen Mary's initiative, to evoke its appearance exactly a century earlier.

155. (above) London Transport poster by Dora Batty featuring Princess Victoria. The poster appeared in 1938, shortly after the opening of the Victorian rooms created by Queen Mary.

room. The rooms were filled with a collection of furniture, curiosities and ephemera relating to the Queen's life and reign (figs. 154 and 155).

There was almost as much activity in the private apartments of the palace. By the 1930s the palace was so associated with the by then elderly relations of Queen Victoria that the Duke of Windsor (formerly Edward VIII; *r.* 1936) famously branded it 'the aunt heap'. As well as Princesses Louise and Beatrice, Kensington was now home to Victoria's granddaughter the Dowager Marchioness of Milford Haven, who was in residence between 1922 and 1950 (figs. 156, 157 and 158). Another of Queen Victoria's granddaughters, Princess Alice, Countess of Athlone, moved into the palace in 1922 and lived there until 1981 (fig. 159).

156. *(opposite, top left) Queen Victoria Eugenie of Spain and her son Infante Jaime at Kensington Palace,* c. *1920. Victoria Eugenie was the daughter of Princess Beatrice and granddaughter of Queen Victoria.*

157. *(opposite, top right)* Princess Beatrice, When Widow to Prince Henry of Battenberg *by Philip Alexius de László, 1926.*

158. *(opposite, bottom left) Wedding photograph of Crown Prince Gustaf Adolf (later Gustaf VI Adolf) of Sweden and Lady Louise Mountbatten (great-granddaughter of Queen Victoria), Kensington Palace, 1923. Louise's mother, the Dowager Marchioness of Milford Haven, was a resident of the palace in the mid-twentieth century.*

159. *(opposite, bottom right) Princess Alice, Countess of Athlone, granddaughter of Queen Victoria. Undated photograph by Hay Wrightson.*

160. *(left) Film still from British Pathé's newsreel 'Famous Buildings Bombed', showing the burnt-out top floors of Apartments 4, 5 and 9 after the incendiary-bomb fire of 14 October 1940.*

161. *(below) Bomb damage to the north range of Clock Court and adjoining parts of the Queen's Apartments, 1940. Shortages of money and materials after the war meant that repairs to some areas had to wait for more than thirty years.*

162. The restoration of the ceiling paintings by Sir Peter Paul Rubens from the Banqueting House at Whitehall was carried out in the Orangery at Kensington Palace from 1945.

163. (right) Series of crown frames, exhibited as part of a display of coronation costume at the London Museum, Kensington Palace, in 1973.

164. (far right) Georgian shopfront from 181 High Holborn, acquired by the London Museum in about 1913. It is shown here in 1952, shortly after the reopening of the museum at Kensington Palace.

The public side of the palace was briefly closed at the start of the Second World War in 1939, but reopened again from 1940 to 1944. The palace suffered considerable damage during the war, with bombs gutting the Queen's Drawing Room and part of the north range of Clock Court (figs. 160 and 161). Even though Britain was in a period of extreme financial austerity, it was unanimously agreed that the State Apartments at Kensington Palace should be restored and reopened to the public as soon as possible; however, some repairs to other parts of the palace had to wait for more than thirty years.

Meanwhile, Princess's Beatrice's former apartment on the floor below was used to house the London Museum, the pre-war home of which, Lancaster House, had been requisitioned by the Foreign Office with no promise of its return. The new museum opened in 1951 with a significantly enlarged collection and four years later expanded into the State Apartments (figs. 163, 164 and 165). The paintings in the state rooms were rearranged, the King's Gallery was redecorated, the ceiling canvases were restored and a range of royal costumes put on display (figs. 166 and 167). Educational activities expanded, too, and by 1965 the palace was welcoming 1200 school parties a year, in addition to more than 290,000 visitors. The museum also played an active role in London's archaeology and ran a lively programme of temporary

165. Her Majesty Queen Elizabeth II inspecting a small glass statuette of Queen Victoria and Prince Albert during her visit to the London Museum at Kensington Palace, 28 November 1956.

166. (right) During the restoration of the King's Gallery ceiling paintings in 1956, the signatures of William Kent and two of his assistants were found on the reverse of the canvases.

167. (below) The King's Gallery after the 1956 restoration work, as used by the London Museum for the display of pictures and costume.

exhibitions. The first of these, in 1954, was *The London of Dickens*, which was followed in 1958 by *The London of Queen Elizabeth I* to mark the 400th anniversary of her accession.

By 1960, however, the museum had again outgrown Kensington. A plan was therefore made to amalgamate the London Museum with the Guildhall Museum and to remove the museum's collection to purpose-built premises in the City. In 1975 the galleries at Kensington were closed, and the Museum of London opened in its new buildings at London Wall in the following year.

But Kensington's role as a museum was not yet over. In the early 1980s a private individual, Aubrey Bowden, offered the long-term loan of his unique collection of court uniforms to Her Majesty The Queen on the understanding that it would be displayed to the public. The former museum rooms at Kensington still lay empty, so were an obvious choice. A curator was appointed, other gifts of clothing were received, and the museum was established as the Court Dress Collection (soon renamed the Royal Ceremonial Dress Collection; fig. 168). The collection, which has since moved to Hampton Court, rapidly grew and now comprises more than 9000 items of dress, from the Tudor period to the late twentieth century, including several items of clothing worn by Queen Victoria. There is a dedicated curator of the collection, and it is also cared for by the Conservation and Collection Care team.

168. Full dress second-class uniform worn by George Irby, 6th Baron Boston, in 1885, one of the many spectacular items of dress in the Royal Ceremonial Dress Collection.

Modern Royals

In the second half of the twentieth century and in the twenty-first, royal life at Kensington Palace has played an important part in the debates about the monarchy and its role in modern Britain. Press exposés and publications have fuelled popular fascination with royal life behind the palace's closed doors, and have sometimes highlighted the stark contrast between the public mask and the private person.

In July 1947, Philip, Prince of Greece and Denmark (later His Royal Highness The Duke of Edinburgh) became engaged to Princess Elizabeth (later Her Majesty Queen Elizabeth II). In the months leading up to the wedding, he returned to live with his mother and grandmother, the Dowager Marchioness of Milford Haven, at Kensington in rooms that were 'astonishingly poor and humble – not at all what one would expect in a palace' (fig. 169). Kensington was also to be Princess Elizabeth and Prince Philip's temporary first home after their marriage, while the bomb damage to their London residence, Clarence House, was being repaired.

The palace was in the spotlight once more when, in 1956, Princess Marina, the glamorous and beautiful widow of the late Prince George, Duke of Kent, and her children, moved into a suite of newly restored rooms in part of Princess Louise's former apartment (figs. 171 and

169. His Royal Highness Prince Philip, Duke of Edinburgh, leaving Kensington Palace on the day of his wedding to Princess Elizabeth on 20 November 1947.

170. Prince Charles and Princess Diana in the drawing room of Apartments 8 and 9, Kensington Palace, in 1985.

171. Princess Marina photographed by Cecil Beaton in 1956 in the hall of her apartment at Kensington Palace, standing in front of Philip Alexius de László's portrait of her mother, Princess Nicholas of Greece and Denmark, Grand Duchess of Russia.

172. (left) Princess Marina (centre) and companions outside the palace during the fire that broke out on 10 January 1963, and which delayed the completion of Princess Margaret and Lord Snowdon's new apartment. Princess Marina married George V's fourth son, George, Duke of Kent, in 1934, and had an apartment at Kensington from 1956 until her death in 1968.

173. (above) Princess Alexandra (daughter of Princess Marina and Prince George, Duke of Kent) and Angus Ogilvy photographed on the announcement of their engagement at Kensington Palace, 30 November 1962.

172). The Princess would live there until her death in 1968, from an inoperable brain tumour, and during that time hosted many official and domestic royal functions (fig. 173).

In 1960 Princess Margaret, sister of Her Majesty Queen Elizabeth II, moved into Kensington with her new husband, Antony Armstrong-Jones, later 1st Earl of Snowdon (figs. 174 and 175). They occupied Apartment 10 (dubbed 'the doll's house' by the Princess) until the refurbishment – which they closely superintended – of their permanent and altogether larger home in Apartment 1A had been completed (fig. 178).

174. (top, left) Lord Snowdon photographed by Cecil Beaton in his study at Kensington Palace in 1965 with his state-of-the art hi-fi and film projector. Films were projected through a hatch in the study wall into the drawing room next door.

175. (top, right) Princess Margaret photographed by Cecil Beaton in her garden at Kensington Palace in 1965.

176. (above) Princess Margaret and Lord Snowdon had a wide circle of celebrity friends, including Peter Sellers and his wife Britt Ekland, shown here in April 1965.

177. (right) Princess Margaret and Lord Snowdon with their children, David and Sarah, in Clock Court. Photograph by Cecil Beaton, 1965.

Beautiful, stylish, intelligent and strong-willed, Margaret was widely viewed as something of a royal rebel. Her romance with Group Captain Peter Townsend, the married equerry of her father, George VI (1936–52), had caused a scandal, and her whirlwind courtship and marriage to the unconventional Armstrong-Jones had been the subject of intense publicity.

178. Photograph of the kitchen in Apartment 1A, showing the trumpet-shaped cooker hood designed by Lord Snowdon.

Princess Margaret enjoyed a dazzling social life and was friends with some of the most famous actors, singers and musicians of the age. Noël Coward, Elizabeth Taylor, Frank Sinatra, Peter Sellers and his wife Britt Ekland were among the attendees at the numerous parties that she and her husband staged at their stylish new apartment at Kensington (fig. 176).

Apartment 1A was also a family home. The couple's son, David, had been born the year after the wedding, and in May 1964 Princess Margaret gave birth to their second child, Lady Sarah, at Kensington (fig. 177). But by now cracks had already begun to appear in the Snowdons' marriage, and by the early 1970s they were living virtually separate lives. In 1978 they finally divorced, the first couple at the centre of the royal family to do so since the reign of Henry VIII.

Princess Margaret continued to live at Kensington until her death in February 2002 (fig. 179). Her coffin lay in the bedroom of her apartment, surrounded by flowers and candles, for two days before it was conveyed to Windsor for the funeral.

179. Princess Margaret in the study of Apartment 1A at Kensington Palace in 1988.

Twenty years before the Princess's death, Kensington became home to one of the most iconic royal couples of modern times: Charles and Diana, Prince and Princess of Wales (figs. 170 and 180). The couple moved into Apartments 8 and 9 in May 1982, by which time Diana was the world's most photographed woman. Her beauty, style and charisma made her the perfect fairy-tale bride for the 'most eligible bachelor in the world'. An estimated 750 million viewers worldwide had tuned in to watch their wedding at St Paul's Cathedral in July 1981.

Diana soon realized that she could use her influence to change public attitudes towards important issues of the day, and she became an active patron of numerous charities. Her natural empathy, warmth and approachability were very different from the public perception of formal royal dignity, and won her widespread admiration. The Princess of Wales was also a fashion icon; her clothes were widely reported and copied, while changes to her hairstyle made front-page news.

Just one month after the Waleses' move to Kensington, their first son, Prince William, was born at St Mary's Hospital in Paddington. Large crowds gathered to see the baby Prince's first appearance, and Princess Margaret organized a welcome reception on their return to the palace. Two years later, their second son, Prince Henry (known

180. (above) Watercolour by Sir Hugh Casson of the entrance to the Prince and Princess of Wales's home at Kensington Palace, presented to the couple by the Royal Institute of British Architects in 1981.

181. (right) Princess Diana with Prince William and Prince Harry, playing on the piano in their home at Kensington Palace in 1985.

182. (left) Princess Diana with David and Elizabeth Emanuel (who designed her wedding dress) in the sitting room of the Waleses' apartment at Kensington, choosing fabrics for her forthcoming royal tour in 1986.

183. (below) Princess Margaret, Prince Charles and Princes William and Harry awaiting the arrival of Queen Beatrix and Prince Claus of The Netherlands outside the Orangery at Kensington Palace in June 1989.

as Harry), was born on 15 September. As Princess Diana wrote: 'The reaction to our small son's arrival has been totally overwhelming – having been sent millions of pink (!) clothes for the last nine months.' At Kensington both Charles and Diana took an active role in bringing up William and Harry with help from their nanny, Barbara Barnes. With her devotion to her sons and her determination that they should have as 'normal' a family life as possible, Princess Diana was hailed as a very modern royal mother (fig. 181).

As their official London home, Kensington was also very much a place of work for the Prince and Princess. From here, they would plan their tours and public engagements, conduct audiences with visiting dignitaries, and hold meetings with officials from the various charities that they supported (figs. 182 and 183). In 1985 the couple broke with tradition and gave their first major television interview in their Kensington Palace apartment. The interview, with ITN's Sir Alastair Burnet, was planned to satisfy the huge demand for TV appearances of the royal couple and to express the importance of their public duties, as well as their commitment to family life. The programme was watched by 20 million viewers in Britain alone.

Despite this show of solidarity, by 1987 it was clear to those close to Prince Charles and Princess Diana that their marriage was falling apart. Diana's equerry, Patrick Jephson, observed that Kensington Palace 'was the backdrop to a dying marriage and its walls had heard too many angry words'. Rumours of a rift between the couple began to appear in the papers, culminating in what has been termed the 'War of the Waleses'.

The couple's life at Kensington was now subject to unprecedented scrutiny by the press. Diana collaborated with the journalist and author Andrew Morton by making a series of tape recordings at Kensington Palace that he serialized in the *Sunday Times* and published as the book *Diana: Her True Story* in June 1992. It caused a sensation: the couple's marriage was portrayed as a constant battle in which the Princess desperately struggled to cope with her husband's indifference and infidelity, while also allegedly receiving no support from the royal family. By December of that year, the Prince and Princess had agreed to separate, and Prince Charles moved out of Kensington Palace.

For the next five years, Princess Diana lived at Kensington Palace alone, apart from when Prince William and Prince Harry stayed with her. Throughout this time, new revelations about her marriage continued to appear in the media. In 1994 Prince Charles agreed to take part in a television documentary in which he spoke frankly about his marriage. But the most sensational exposé about their relationship came from the Princess herself, who in the following year agreed to an interview at Kensington Palace with Martin Bashir for the BBC programme *Panorama*. The interview became one of the television events of the decade and attracted an audience of almost 23 million. It also prompted The Queen to tell her son and daughter-in-law that they should divorce, which they did in 1996.

In what would be the last year of her life, Diana threw herself into her humanitarian work. She visited Angola and Bosnia to campaign with the Red Cross against landmines, and auctioned seventy-nine of her gowns in New York, raising £3 million for AIDS and cancer charities. A number of these dresses are now in the Royal Ceremonial Dress Collection.

Diana's death in a car accident in Paris with her partner, Dodi Fayed, on 31 August 1997 stunned the world and provoked an unprecedented wave of national mourning in which Kensington Palace played a central part. In the days that followed, the public converged on Kensington Gardens and laid thousands of floral tributes at the iconic golden gates (fig. 184). Floral tributes are still laid at the gates to mark each anniversary of the Princess's death (fig. 185).

Today the palace remains closely associated with Princess Diana and the public interest, praise and criticism that shaped her life to an unprecedented degree. A positive legacy is that press coverage of royal private life at Kensington Palace has been less intrusive since her death.

Kensington is still one of the principal residences of the royal family. Although London and its surrounds have changed a great deal since the palace was first built, Kensington even now boasts both a convenient central location and seclusion, thanks to the surrounding gardens and park.

The Duke and Duchess of Gloucester continue to occupy Apartment 1, in the south-western corner of Clock Court, where they have lived since their marriage in 1972. From 1994 until her death in 2004, the Duke's mother, Princess Alice, Duchess of Gloucester, shared the apartment with them. She became the oldest ever member of the royal family in August 2003, superseding Her Majesty The Queen Mother's record-breaking 101 years and 238 days. On her death at the age of 102, one commentator in *The Guardian* remarked, 'She was perhaps the last great Edwardian lady; the final echo of a world and social order, now long gone.'

184. The sea of flowers and other tributes placed at the South Front of Kensington Palace in the days after the death of Diana, Princess of Wales, on 31 August 1997.

185. The White Garden, created in the Sunken Garden in 2017 to mark the twentieth anniversary of the death of Diana, Princess of Wales.

186. (right) The Duke and Duchess of Cambridge, Prince George and Princess Charlotte in the garden of Apartment 1A at Kensington Palace in 2015.

187. (below) In April 2016 the Duke and Duchess of Cambridge and Prince Harry hosted an informal dinner for the President of the United States of America, Barack Obama, and his wife, Michelle. The President is photographed here in the drawing room of the Cambridges' apartment at Kensington Palace. The two-year-old Prince George is wearing his dressing gown, ready for bed.

Prince Edward, Duke of Kent, and his younger brother, Prince Michael, also returned to live at Kensington Palace, having originally shared Apartment 1 during the 1950s and '60s with their mother, Princess Marina. In 1978, after his marriage to the Czech-born Baroness Marie-Christine von Reibnitz, Prince Michael was allocated Apartment 10, in the north-eastern corner of the palace.

By far the most famous of Kensington's modern royal residents, however, are the Duke and Duchess of Cambridge and their children (fig. 186). In 2011, shortly after their marriage, Prince William, by then Duke of Cambridge, returned to live at his childhood home with his wife, Catherine. Initially, they moved into Nottingham Cottage while Princess Margaret's former apartment, 1A, was extensively renovated, transforming it into their new home. The work was completed in 2014, and since then the apartment has been the Duke and Duchess of Cambridge's principal residence and a family home for themselves and their three children, Prince George, Princess Charlotte and Prince Louis.

Prince Harry (now the Duke of Sussex) also returned to live at Kensington Palace, taking up residence in the Cambridges' former home, Nottingham Cottage. In November 2017 he and his then fiancée, Meghan Markle, posed for photographs in the Sunken Garden after the announcement of their engagement (fig. 188).

The Duke and Duchess of Cambridge and Prince Harry have received a number of official visitors at Kensington, as well as representatives of the many charities that they support. In April 2016 they hosted an informal dinner in Apartment 1A for the President of the United States of America, Barack Obama, and his wife, Michelle (fig. 187). This was the first time that the Cambridges and Prince Harry had entertained a head of state privately, and the most significant event that they have hosted at Kensington Palace.

188. Prince Harry and Meghan Markle announced their engagement in November 2017 and posed for official photographs in the Sunken Garden at Kensington Palace. After their marriage in 2018, they took up residence in the Prince's home, Nottingham Cottage, in the grounds of Kensington Palace.

The Palace Today

In 1989 the Historic Royal Palaces Agency (HRPA) was formed in response to a government inquiry into a devastating fire at Hampton Court Palace three years earlier. This called for a more streamlined and effective management system for Hampton Court, the public side of Kensington Palace, the Tower of London, Kew Palace and the Banqueting House at Whitehall. HRPA was to have a greater level of autonomy from central government, and under its management the interests of the unoccupied royal palaces were brought together for the first time.

During the decade that followed, the agency undertook major re-presentations, improved the visitor experience and realized

189. (right) The 'Wiggly Walk', a new garden feature created during the 'Welcome to Kensington' project in 2012. The curving paths recall the 'wiggly walks' of the gardens laid out for Queen Caroline in the 1720s and '30s.

190. (opposite) The 'Temple of the Four Great Monarchies of the World', made by Charles Clay, Clockmaker to the Board of Works, and completed by John Pyke in 1743. It was installed in the Cupola Room (shown here) during the reign of George III, removed in the early nineteenth century and reinstated there in 1994 on a plinth re-created after an eighteenth-century engraving.

191. Dresses belonging to Queen Elizabeth II, including gowns by Sir Norman Hartnell and Sir Hardy Amies, on display at Kensington Palace in 1998.

the commercial potential of the palaces. The legacy of this was the transformation in 1998 of HRPA into Historic Royal Palaces (HRP), the independent charity that continues to manage the five unoccupied royal palaces, together with Hillsborough Castle, Her Majesty The Queen's official residence in Northern Ireland.

The impact of these administrative changes on Kensington has been profound. During the 1990s, a major restoration of the State Apartments was carried out in order to return them to their appearance during the reign of George I. Meanwhile, the Victorian rooms were preserved as an interesting re-presentation of a key period in the palace's history and as an example of Queen Mary's curatorial input.

All of this work was based on meticulous archival research and the commissioning of high-quality and accurate replica objects, in order to restore, as far as possible, the palace's historic appearance and atmosphere. It also set the standard for the next major project undertaken by Historic Royal Palaces: 'Welcome to Kensington: A

192. (above) There were queues around the block to see the exhibition Diana: Her Fashion Story, *staged at Kensington in 2017–19 to mark the twentieth anniversary of the Princess's death. Several iconic dresses were displayed, including the famous 'Travolta' dress, which Diana wore when she danced with John Travolta at the White House in 1985.*

193. (left) A member of Historic Royal Palaces' Conservation and Collection Care team mounting one of the dresses for the exhibition Diana: Her Fashion Story *in 2017.*

Palace for Everyone'. Its aims were to restore the link between the palace and its landscape in order to reflect their historic relationship; to create accessible new public spaces, free of charge, including a new café and shop; to improve physical access to the palace and educational services for children; to provide a dedicated exhibition space for the Royal Ceremonial Dress Collection (fig. 191); and, most importantly, to tell the history of the palace and the significant events in our nation's history that have taken place there (fig. 189).

On 15 March 2012, Her Majesty The Queen and the Duke of Edinburgh reopened Kensington Palace and toured the newly presented rooms. Over the following months visitor numbers soared, with around 20,000 people a week visiting in the first month alone.

Since then, visitor figures have remained buoyant, thanks in no small part to the programme of exhibitions that have been staged at the palace. The 2012 project included the creation of a dedicated exhibition space, the Pigott Galleries, which have played host to a series of hugely popular displays. Most of these have been on themes relating to royal dress, with many items being drawn from the ever-expanding Royal Ceremonial Dress Collection. The *Fashion Rules* exhibition in 2013 and its sequel three years later included dresses worn by Her Majesty The Queen, Princess Margaret and Princess Diana. In 2017 Kensington launched the enormously popular *Diana: Her Fashion Story*, an exhibition of the Princess's dresses to mark the

194. Enlightened Princesses: Caroline, Augusta, Charlotte, and the Shaping of the Modern World, *a collaboration between Historic Royal Palaces and the Yale Center for British Art, opened at Kensington Palace in June 2017. The exhibition explored the lives of three German princesses, all of whom married into the British royal family in the eighteenth century, and their wide-ranging intellectual, social and political interests.*

twentieth anniversary of her death (figs. 192 and 193). Kensington has gained greater renown for its exhibitions than any of the other Historic Royal Palaces (fig. 194).

The work of Historic Royal Palaces at Kensington Palace is far from complete. Since 2012 further significant improvements have been made to the King's State Apartments, including the installation of oak floorboards, replica crimson silk hangings in the Presence Chamber and the return in these rooms of some furniture made for George II by the London firm of Gumley and Moore.

An ambitious programme of further conservation, restoration and public-engagement work is planned for other parts of the palace in future years. All of this will help to ensure that Kensington's history – as both a visitor attraction and a living palace – will continue to evolve. The story of the palace has many more chapters to come.

Family Tree

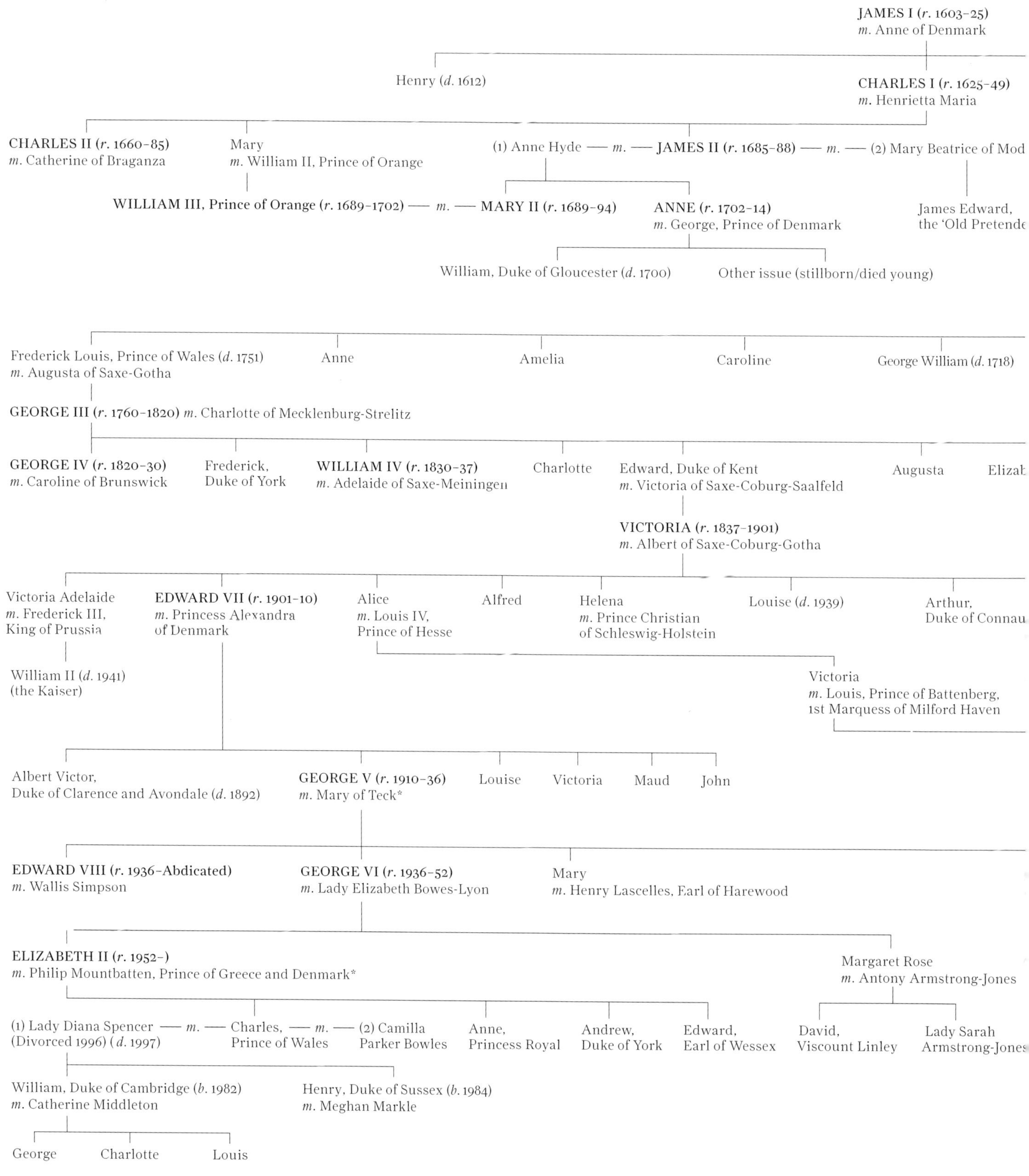
JAMES I (r. 1603–25)
m. Anne of Denmark
Henry (d. 1612)
CHARLES I (r. 1625–49)
m. Henrietta Maria
CHARLES II (r. 1660–85)
m. Catherine of Braganza
Mary
m. William II, Prince of Orange
(1) Anne Hyde — m. — JAMES II (r. 1685–88) — m. — (2) Mary Beatrice of Mod
WILLIAM III, Prince of Orange (r. 1689–1702) — m. — MARY II (r. 1689–94)
ANNE (r. 1702–14)
m. George, Prince of Denmark
James Edward,
the 'Old Pretende
William, Duke of Gloucester (d. 1700)
Other issue (stillborn/died young)
Frederick Louis, Prince of Wales (d. 1751)
m. Augusta of Saxe-Gotha
Anne
Amelia
Caroline
George William (d. 1718)
GEORGE III (r. 1760–1820) m. Charlotte of Mecklenburg-Strelitz
GEORGE IV (r. 1820–30)
m. Caroline of Brunswick
Frederick,
Duke of York
WILLIAM IV (r. 1830–37)
m. Adelaide of Saxe-Meiningen
Charlotte
Edward, Duke of Kent
m. Victoria of Saxe-Coburg-Saalfeld
Augusta
Elizab
VICTORIA (r. 1837–1901)
m. Albert of Saxe-Coburg-Gotha
Victoria Adelaide
m. Frederick III,
King of Prussia
EDWARD VII (r. 1901–10)
m. Princess Alexandra
of Denmark
Alice
m. Louis IV,
Prince of Hesse
Alfred
Helena
m. Prince Christian
of Schleswig-Holstein
Louise (d. 1939)
Arthur,
Duke of Connau
William II (d. 1941)
(the Kaiser)
Victoria
m. Louis, Prince of Battenberg,
1st Marquess of Milford Haven
Albert Victor,
Duke of Clarence and Avondale (d. 1892)
GEORGE V (r. 1910–36)
m. Mary of Teck*
Louise
Victoria
Maud
John
EDWARD VIII (r. 1936–Abdicated)
m. Wallis Simpson
GEORGE VI (r. 1936–52)
m. Lady Elizabeth Bowes-Lyon
Mary
m. Henry Lascelles, Earl of Harewood
ELIZABETH II (r. 1952–)
m. Philip Mountbatten, Prince of Greece and Denmark*
Margaret Rose
m. Antony Armstrong-Jones
(1) Lady Diana Spencer — m. — Charles, — m. — (2) Camilla
(Divorced 1996) (d. 1997)
Prince of Wales
Parker Bowles
Anne,
Princess Royal
Andrew,
Duke of York
Edward,
Earl of Wessex
David,
Viscount Linley
Lady Sarah
Armstrong-Jones
William, Duke of Cambridge (b. 1982)
m. Catherine Middleton
Henry, Duke of Sussex (b. 1984)
m. Meghan Markle
George
Charlotte
Louis

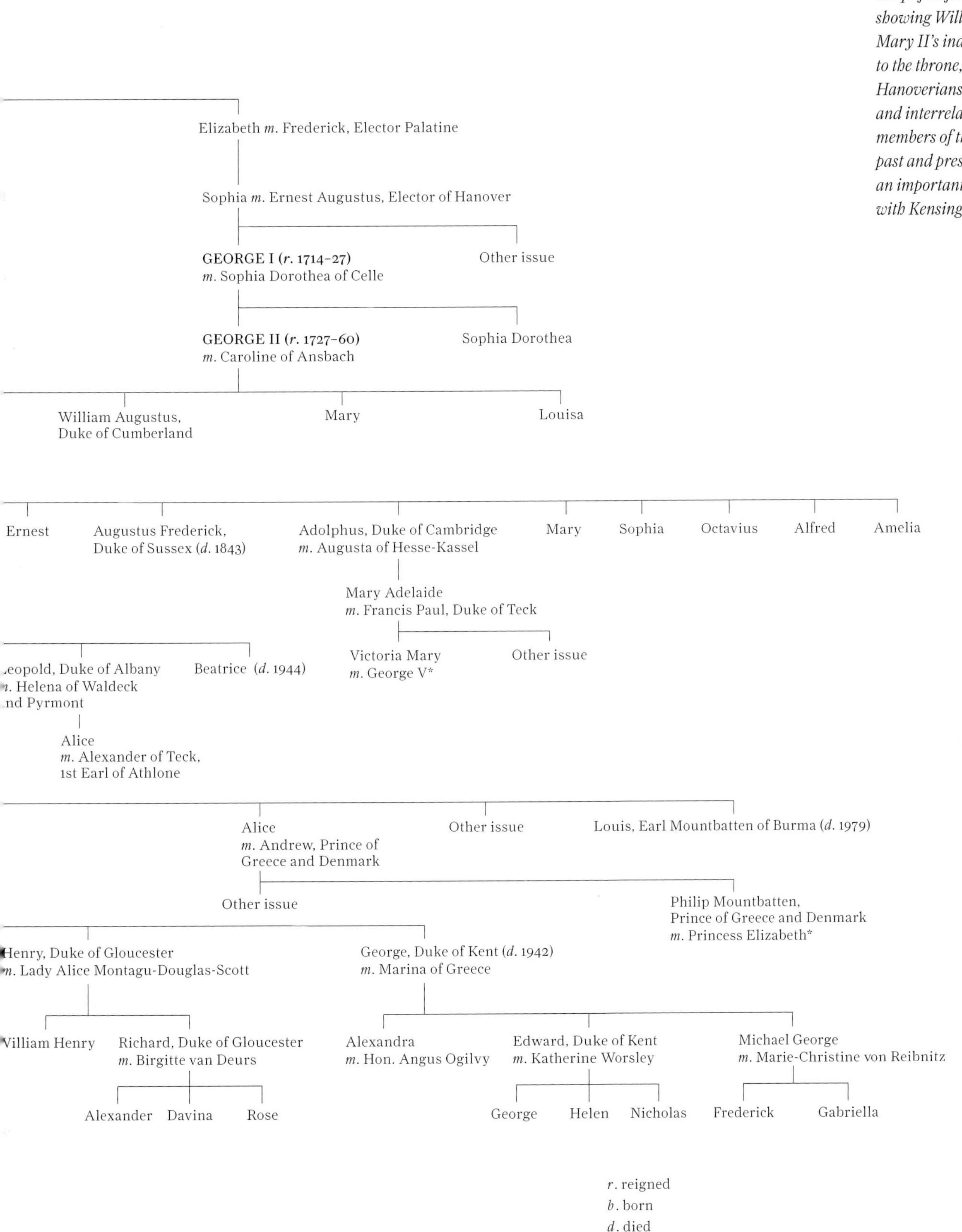

Simplified family tree showing William III and Mary II's individual claims to the throne, that of the Hanoverians, and the descent and interrelationship of members of the royal family, past and present, who have an important association with Kensington Palace.

r. reigned
b. born
d. died
* see elsewhere on family tree

Further Reading

Tracy Borman, *Henrietta Howard: King's Mistress, Queen's Servant*, London (Jonathan Cape) 2007

H.M. Colvin (ed.), *The History of the King's Works*, vol. V (1976) and vol. VI (1973), London (HMSO)

Thomas Faulkner, *History and Antiquities of Kensington*, London 1820

Olivia Fryman *et al.*, *Kensington Palace: Art, Architecture and Society*, New Haven, Conn., and London (Yale University Press) 2018

John Hervey, *Lord Hervey's Memoirs*, ed. Romney Sedgwick, London (William Kimber) 1952

Mark Hinton and Oliver Impey (eds.), *Kensington Palace and the Porcelain of Queen Mary II*, London (Christie's in collaboration with the Ashmolean Museum, Oxford, and Historic Royal Palaces) 1998

Edward Impey, *Kensington Palace: The Official Illustrated History*, rev. edn, London (Merrell/Historic Royal Palaces) 2012

Deirdre Murphy, *The Young Victoria*, New Haven, Conn., and London (Yale University Press) 2019

David Souden with Lucy Worsley and Brett Dolman, *The Royal Palaces of London*, London (Merrell/Historic Royal Palaces) 2008

Acknowledgements

I would like to express my thanks to all of my colleagues at Historic Royal Palaces upon whose advice, expertise and support I have been able to draw. I am particularly grateful to the Publishing Manager, Clare Murphy, for her incredibly hard work in managing the project, providing editorial guidance and, along with Annie Heron, producing such inspired picture research. Many thanks are also due to James Brittain for his wonderful photography. I am indebted to the authors of the major new scholarly history of the palace: Olivia Fryman, Sebastian Edwards, Joanna Marschner, Deirdre Murphy and Lee Prosser. I was also fortunate to draw on the scholarship of Dr Edward Impey, author of the predecessor of this book, *Kensington Palace: The Official Illustrated History*.

My thanks are due to the curatorial team at Kensington Palace, notably Claudia Williams and Isabella Coraça, as well as to Eleri Lynn, Dress Curator, for her invaluable insights into the Royal Ceremonial Dress Collection. I am grateful to Sebastian Edwards, Head of Collections, for his editorial help, and to Adrian Phillips, Palaces and Collections Director, for giving me the time to complete the book. My friend and fellow historian John Moses was kind enough to share his research on the architectural history of the palace with me.

The team at Merrell have, as ever, been assiduous throughout. I would particularly like to thank Claire Chandler for her meticulous editing, Nicola Bailey for design and Elizabeth of Mar for publicity, as well as Hugh Merrell for commissioning the book.

When it was originally conceived, this book was to have been jointly authored with Deirdre Murphy, Senior Curator at Kensington Palace. Tragically, Deirdre was unable to fulfil the project because she was diagnosed with terminal cancer. She passed away in May 2018, aged forty-two. This book is dedicated to her memory.

Tracy Borman
July 2018

Picture Credits

Alamy: figs. 176 (Trinity Mirror/Mirrorpix), 179 (Jayne Fincher.Photo Int); The Warden and Fellows of All Souls College, Oxford: fig. 54; Barbara Allwood: fig. 126; © Bomann-Museum, Celle: fig. 53; Bridgeman Images: back jacket/cover bottom left (private collection), p. 5 top (private collection), figs. 42 (By permission of the British Library), 46 (private collection/Stapleton Collection), 52 (Lebrecht Music and Arts), 77 (private collection), 86 (private collection), 127 (private collection), 142 (private collection), 143 (private collection), 144 (private collection), 158 (photo © Collection Gregoire); By permission of the British Library: fig. 83; © The Trustees of The British Museum: figs. 15, 44, 55, 85, 88, 95, 106; British Pathé: fig. 160; Camera Press, London: p. 5 centre (Cecil Beaton), figs. 174 (Cecil Beaton), 175 (Cecil Beaton), 177 (Cecil Beaton); The Devonshire Collection, Chatsworth. Reproduced by permission of the Chatsworth Settlement Trustees: figs. 25, 56; A.E. Henson/Country Life Picture Library: fig. 70; Getty Images: figs. 31, 73 (Jason Hawkes), 146 (Central Press), 156 (© Hulton-Deutsch Collection/Corbis), 165 (Popperfoto), 169 (Popperfoto), 170 (Tim Graham), 181 (Tim Graham), 182 (Tim Graham), 184 (Peter Turnley/Corbis), 187 (Pete Souza/The White House), 188 (Daniel Leal-Olivas/AFP); Paleis Het Loo, Apeldoorn, Eelco Boeijinga: fig. 13; Historic England Archive: figs. 78 (Audley End), 92, 161; © Historic Royal Palaces www.images.hrp.org.uk: front jacket/cover, back jacket/cover top left and right, back jacket/cover bottom right (© David Jensen), front endpaper/inside front cover (plan by Daphne Ford), back endpaper/inside back cover, frontispiece, pp. 4 top, 6–7, 152–53, figs. 1, 2, 3, 4, 6, 7, 10 (Will Foster Illustration) 26 (Crown copyright), 27, 28, 29, 30, 33, 34 (Will Foster Illustration), 35 (Will Foster Illustration), 36, 37, 39, 40, 50, 58, 59, 60, 61, 62, 63, 64, 65, 66, 67, 68, 69, 82, 90, 91, 93, 96, 102, 107, 114, 117, 124, 130, 131, 134 (Crown copyright), 138, 139, 140 (Crown copyright), 141, 148, 149, 154, 155, 162 (Crown copyright), 164 (Crown copyright), 166 (Crown copyright), 167 (Crown copyright), 168, 178, 185, 189, 190, 191 (© David Jensen), 192 (Richard Lea-Hair), 193 (Richard Lea-Hair), 194 (© SWNS); © Courtesy of The Huntington Art Collections, San Marino, California: figs. 12 (51.13), 89 (ST Map 147); © Imperial War Museum: fig. 153 (IWM_ART_004734); © Chris Jelf: p. 5 bottom, fig. 186; The Royal Borough of Kensington and Chelsea Library and Arts Services: figs. 9, 87, 133; Mary Evans Picture Library: figs. 145, 152, 159 (Hay Wrightson); Museum of London: figs. 147, 150, 151, 163; © The National Archives (PRO): figs. 8 (E 31/2/1, f. 130v), 21 (Work 5/146), 79 (Work 34/118), 115 (Work 34/717), 132 (Work 34/734); National Monuments Record: figs. 72, 136; © National Portrait Gallery, London: p. 4 centre, figs. 5, 11, 14, 41, 49, 51, 57, 80, 81, 100, 113; The Pepys Library, Magdalene College, Cambridge: fig. 22; Rex Features: figs. 172, 183 (Peter Turnley); Royal Collection Trust/© Her Majesty Queen Elizabeth II 2019: p. 4 bottom, figs. 16, 17, 18, 20, 23, 24, 32, 38, 43, 45, 71, 74, 76, 84, 94, 97, 98, 99, 101, 103, 104, 108, 109, 110, 111, 112, 116, 119, 120, 121, 122, 123, 125, 128, 129, 137, 157; © The Royal Society: fig. 19; © Sir John Soane's Museum, London: fig. 48; © Kupferstich-Kabinett, Staatliche Kunstsammlungen Dresden (photo: Andreas Diesend): fig. 105; © Tate, London 2019: fig. 118; © TopFoto: figs. 135, 173 (PA Photos); © Victoria and Albert Museum, London: figs. 75, 171; Reproduced by kind permission of His Royal Highness The Prince of Wales: fig. 180; © Warwick Castle: fig. 47

The publishers have made every effort to trace and contact copyright holders of the illustrations reproduced in this book; they shall be happy to correct in subsequent editions any errors or omissions that are brought to their attention.

Index

Page numbers in *italic* refer to the illustrations.

First published 2019 by Merrell Publishers, London and New York

Merrell Publishers Limited
70 Cowcross Street
London EC1M 6EJ
merrellpublishers.com

in association with

Historic Royal Palaces
Hampton Court Palace
Surrey KT8 9AU
hrp.org.uk

British Library Cataloguing in Publication Data. A catalogue record for this book is available from the British Library.

ISBN 978-1-8589-4674-0 (hardback)
ISBN 978-1-8589-4677-1 (paperback)

Produced by Merrell Publishers Limited
Designed by Nicola Bailey
Project-managed by Claire Chandler
Proofread by Barbara Roby
Indexed by Hilary Bird

Printed and bound in China

Front jacket/cover: The South Front of Kensington Palace.

Back jacket/cover, clockwise from top left: The East Front of Kensington Palace, with Princess Louise's statue of Queen Victoria in the foreground (detail of fig. 130); The King's Staircase, created by William Kent between 1725 and 1727 (see fig. 67); Dresses belonging to Queen Elizabeth II on display at Kensington Palace in 1998 (detail of fig. 191); Illustration by Arthur Rackham for J.M. Barrie's Peter Pan in Kensington Gardens, *1906 (detail of fig. 143).*

Back endpaper/inside back cover: The ceiling of the Cupola Room, painted by William Kent in 1722 (detail of fig. 59).

Frontispiece: The Privy Chamber, one of Queen Caroline's favourite entertaining spaces. Arranged around the room are marble busts of her contemporary heroes, commissioned from Giovanni Battista Guelfi.

Pages 4–5, top to bottom: Detail from the King's Staircase mural depicting Peter the Wild Boy and Dr John Arbuthnot (see fig. 69); Queen Anne with her son, William, Duke of Gloucester, from the studio of Sir Godfrey Kneller, c. *1694 (detail of fig. 41);* Queen Victoria When a Girl *by Alexandre-Jean Dubois Drahonet, 1832 (see fig. 109); Princess Louise, Duchess of Argyll, by Philip Alexius de László, 1915 (see fig. 127); Princess Margaret and Lord Snowdon with their children, David and Sarah, photographed in Clock Court by Cecil Beaton, 1965 (see fig. 177); The Duke and Duchess of Cambridge with Prince George and Princess Charlotte in the garden of their apartment at Kensington Palace, 2015 (detail of fig. 186).*

Pages 6–7: Fallow deer in the royal paddock at Kensington, from a painting attributed to Francis Barlow, c. *1695 (detail of fig. 40).*